THE CENTINELA WEAVERS OF CHIMAYO

UNFOLDING TRADITION

THE CENTINELA WEAVERS OF CHIMAYO UNFOLDING TRADITION

A brief history of weaving in New Mexico's Rio Grande Valley and its development throughout several generations of Trujillos in Chimayó to the present family of weavers.

By Mary Terence McKay and Lisa Trujillo

CENTINELA TRADITIONAL ARTS

CHIMAYO, NEW MEXICO

We would like to acknowledge Mercedes Trujillo and all the other oral interviewees—Jake, Ross, Irvin, and Lisa Trujillo and Pat Trujillo Oviedo—whose personal accounts added dimension to the family history. Additionally, thanks go to Jack Loeffler, who kindly provided tapes of his interviews with Jake; to Ursulo Ortiz, John R. Trujillo, Marin Meir, and Jonathan Batkin for their personal insight; to Helen and Tim Cordova for their commentary; to Helen Lucero, Suzanne Baizerman, and Don Usner for their help and support; and to David Smith for keeping the project from coming to a grinding halt. Our appreciation also to Albino, Ernestine, and Pita Trujillo for contributing their extensive knowledge of our family tree; to the Centinela Traditional Arts staff and others who read this manuscript and offered comments over the course of the project; and to Karen Embertson, who stuck with us despite all the setbacks.

Published by Centinela Traditional Arts
HCR 64, Box 4 Chimayo, NM 87522
www.chimayoweavers.com

ISBN 0-9668862-0-8

Design, project coordinator: Karen Embertson
Photography: Addison Doty: pp. 8, 9, 29, 41, 45, 48, 51, 56, 63, 67, 68, 69, 70, 71, 72, 73A, 75, 77, 78; Richard Wickstrom: pp. 33, 40, 53, 55, 59, 60, 61, 62, 64, 73B, 76; Rod Hook: pp. 35, 46, 54, 58, 74, 79; Carla Breeze: pp. 31, 50, 57; Edward Rice III: p. 52; Steve Northup: p. 81
Chapter graphic from detail of weaving by Dimas Vigil
Printed by CS Graphics, Singapore

Front cover: Mexican Killer Bees *(detail), 1991, by Irvin Trujillo. Commercial 4-ply, natural- and commercial-dyed weft with 2-ply warp, 54 x 84 inches. Collection of Dan and Martha Albrecht.*

Back cover: Pueblo Birds, *1990, by Lisa Trujillo. Commercial 4-ply, natural-dyed and undyed weft with 2-ply warp, 36 x 60 inches. Private collection.*

CONTENTS

PREFACE

by Lisa Trujillo

WHETHER COMING FROM Santa Fe or Taos, the trip to Chimayó will take you from dry, piñon- and juniper-covered hills into a green valley of irrigated fields, shady trees, and modest homes. The change in vegetation is as striking as the number of weaving shops in the town, more than are found in some American cities. Visitors stopping in each of these shops will learn something of what Chimayó weaving looks like, but they would get only a glimpse of its long and varied history and of the broader history of Hispanic weaving in New Mexico's Rio Grande Valley.

As the Chimayó Valley extends eastward from the main part of town it narrows, filling with apple orchards and animal pastures. Here at Centinela Traditional Arts, we are frequently asked how we came to set up shop in this place and about the story behind our weavings. Because we found it difficult, nearly impossible, to provide enough information to people—about how the production of these blankets, historically a local necessity, has survived to become an art form and vital source of income to Chimayosos at the end of the twentieth century, about how much weaving matters to us and our neighbors, and why we have dedicated our lives to such a time-consuming practice—we decided to create this book.

We hope that with this book you will enjoy the beautiful weavings more fully and understand how they've come about and how they differ from those at other shops. This book will allow Irvin and I to keep working at our looms, creating new textiles to please the imagination, the eye, and the soul. Even without the opportunity to wander through Chimayó, the reader can use this book to discover a place far removed from the fast-paced, modern American life dominated by concrete, metal, plastic, and electronics. Our weavings are created primarily of wool and time, and an unflagging spirit born of place and history. We hope the dedication to our craft shines through.

TRUJILLO FAMILY TREE

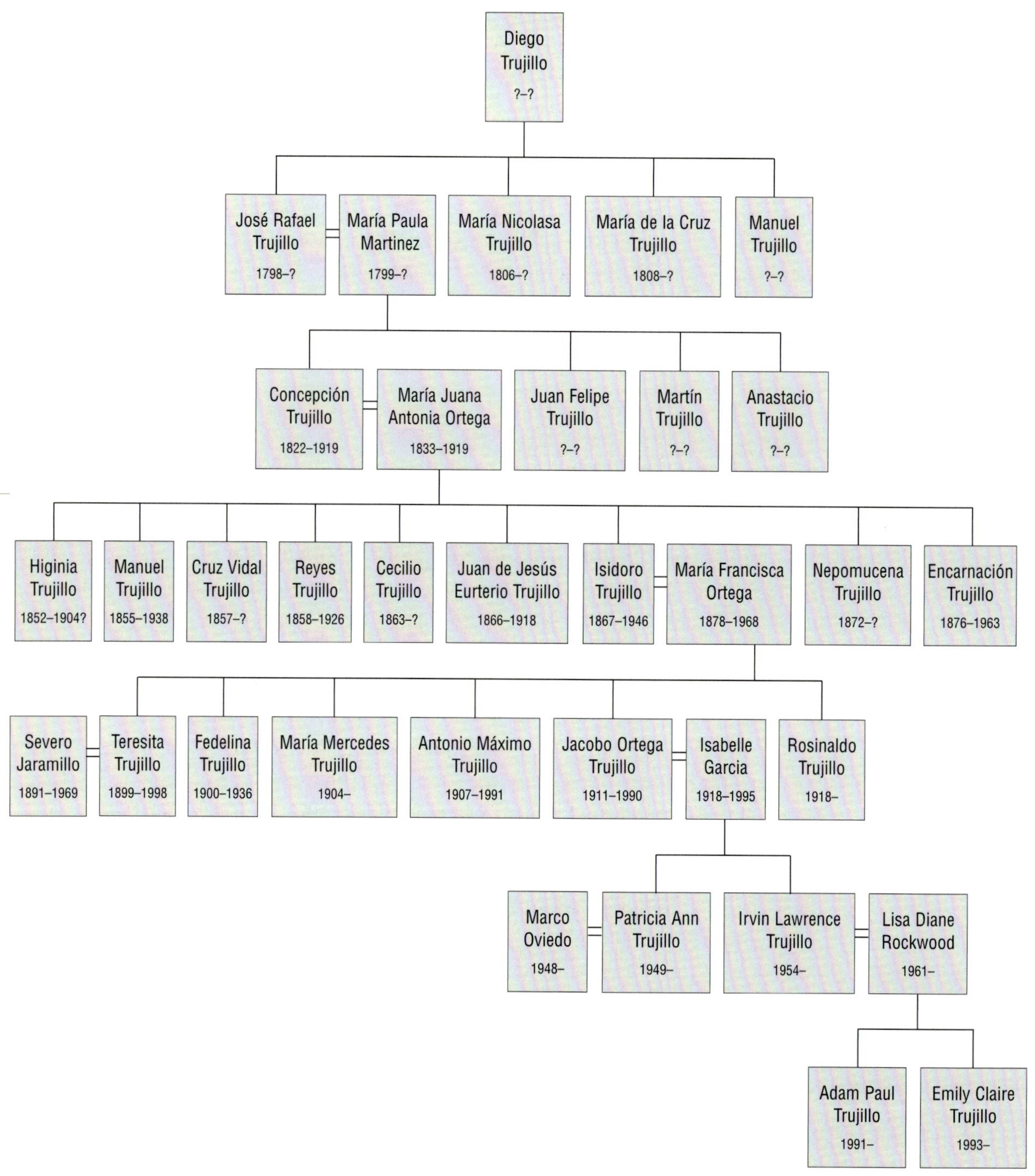

PROLOGUE

Essay in Four Parts
by Mary Terence McKay

AUNTIE MERCEDES'S FLANNEL nightgown enveloped the child, who giggled in anticipation of their nightly ritual—the layering of *frazada* after frazada upon him until the sheer weight of the thick, warm, handspun blankets was almost unbearable. "*No tantos,*" he finally protested, and she ceased her caretaking for the night and crossed back quietly to her room.

The fire, which now burned fiercely, rose up through the opened vents in the door of the *fogón,* stoked minutes earlier with *piñón* and rock coal. Firelight played upon the adobe walls and illuminated every corner of the dark room, which soon became permeated with the sweet incense of burning piñon and the petrolated fumes seeping from the rock coal that would smolder with life until the wee hours of the morning. There had been games and stories and much laughter and finally Grandmother Francisquita's nightly blessing, which always preceded the children's sleep.

Once tall and beautiful (an Ortega before her marriage), in later years Francisquita was still distinguished looking, a refined and gentle woman whose finely chiseled face was framed by clouds of gray-white hair she wore in a chignon and whose eyes seemed to widen and deepen over the years with all the love she bore for others. Her most striking aspect, however, was and had always been her faith in God and her total acceptance of life—of things as they were—of beauty and then darkness.

When the boy was quite young, she would sit at the kitchen table with the others for meals. But later on, when she couldn't walk very well, she stayed in her room praying the rosary and took her meals there on a tray Mercedes, her daughter, would bring to her.

In spite of her blindness, or perhaps because of it, Francisquita loved children and welcomed them around her. Sometimes they played rhyming games such as "Cesto Maestas," the Spanish equivalent of "Eeny Meeny Miny Mo":

> Cesto Maestas / Martín de las Questas
> que dijo mi padre / que asote la questa
> Con una capal / que está en el corral
> Chorro morro / Por este me corro.

Sometimes, though she spoke only Spanish, she mesmerized them with favorite *cuentos* (stories)—"Pedro de Urdimales" or "Marialinda" —and *consejos* (fables) taken from Cervantes's tales, filled with kings and queens on horseback, spectacular feats of magic, and spellbinding images into which she breathed life. These she told as only a blind woman could, with all her senses focused on the telling.

Outside now, well into the Christmas season, icicles scarred with the cracks and fissures of as many thaws and freezes extended their long fingers a good five feet down from the roof of the adobe house toward neat stacks of piñon firewood that rose up to greet them, creating the effect of a rather exotic fortress.

The notion of fortress seemed appropriate for a hacienda nestled at the base of Cuchilla de la Centinela, the sentinel hill and observation point for all of Chimayó, where, from the eighteenth century on, lookouts kept watch for raiding parties of fierce Comanches and others that swept down from the foothills to the east and sometimes from the Cañada Ancha to the northeast to attack a seemingly indefensible settlement of Hispanic homes and an adobe plaza called Chimayó in the heart of the upper Santa Cruz Valley.[1] The town was named for the 7,000-foot *cerro* that dominated it, Tsi Mayoh, Tewa for "hill of the East," one of four sacred hills that described the Tewa world.[2]

Chimayó is an ancient and holy place. Before the Tewas, there were the Anasazi, who arrived a thousand years ago. Their cultural remains, particularly the pottery—with its triangles, interlocking scrolls, and parallel, zigzagging lines of Red Mesa Black-on-white and Chaco Black-on-white—transfigure the valley floor, suggesting a highly advanced people of rich artistic tradition.[3]

The relics of these ancients, the stone-cobbled fire pits and flaked obsidian of the Archaic peoples before them, and the stone weapons and tools of the Paleo-Indians before them imbue the valley with the sacred patina of some ancient reliquary, a patina enhanced by the rose-colored light that seems to have mysteriously and permanently settled over the valley but is, in fact, reflected off the pink granitic bedrock of the Sangre de Cristo Mountains.[4] From the north and south, light glancing off the formidable barrancas only intensifies and clarifies this rubylike setting.[5]

. . . The Northern New Mexico winter night, crystal clear and silent, wrapped itself around the house and settled down to sleep. Inside, the child—young Irvin Trujillo—burrowed deeper into the frazadas and wondered if Grandmother Francisquita had become blind from all the spinning and weaving that she used to do.

ANTEPASADOS Y TIEMPO

THE SPANISH COLONIALS had attached themselves to a military train that traveled north from Mexico City across the volcanic mantle of altiplano called the Mexican Plateau. To the west, its harsh beauty was dissected by deep and angular gorges, the majestic barrancas of the Sierra Madre Occidental; to the east lay the volcanic spires and steep-walled narrow valleys of the Sierra Madre Oriental. Between these ranges on windswept uplands, the train of humanity pressed north to Chihuahua and ever north across the Chihuahuan Desert through ground cover of open mesquite and undergrowth of yucca.

They forded the Rio Grande River at Paso del Norte and continued relentlessly north across the Jornada del Muerto, a grueling two-day passage that took the lives of several weakened by a thousand miles of arduous travel. Finally, they reached a settlement called La Joya de Sevilleta, just south of the Manzano Mountains.[6] Among these colonials from Estremadura, Spain, were Irvin Trujillo's people, lured by the promise of land and riches to settle the "Kingdom of New Mexico" on behalf of the Spanish throne and Holy Mother Church.[7]

Diego de Trujillo, nineteen or twenty years old, who records himself as an *alférez* (second lieutenant) and farmer born in Mexico City, first appeared in New Mexican records in 1632. He enjoyed a notable military career as lieutenant general for the Rio Abajo area and *alcalde* (mayor) of Zuni, and he may be a forebear of Irvin Trujillo.[8] His grandchildren, returning to New Mexico after the Spanish Reconquest in 1693, settled first in the vicinity of Albuquerque and then moved north over the next fifty years.[9]

Had anyone inquired as to their occupation during these early years, they would have identified themselves as settlers first and later as farmers and ranchers, descriptions that followed them well into the twentieth century. Of secondary importance was their role as weavers, for weaving was only one aspect of the rhythm of life on the land. Their economy was a subsistence one; goods were bartered for other goods. These Trujillos probably traded weavings for food and other supplies, but no ancestral Trujillo set himself up as "weaver" and wove for profit.[10]

By approximately 1760, a second Diego—Irvin's great-great-great-grandfather—was living in Rio Chiquito on the road to La Azotea, a mesa that afforded the village protection from the Indians.[11] One of the earliest settlements after De Vargas's reconquest of New Mexico, Rio Chiquito would later become an eastern *placita* of Chimayó, a site where adobe homes clustered together, often indicating an extended family. Today, only the foundations of Diego's dwelling remain, hardly sufficient for one to infer more than a glimpse of a man whose life and livelihood were closely tied to the upper Santa Cruz Valley.

Encarnación Trujillo, Irvin's great-uncle, used to say that Diego had six looms,[12] a matter for speculation among family members today, though there could easily have been Indian servants to augment the labor force. Servant labor was common in the New Mexico Territory, especially in the carding and spinning of wool.[13] In fact, one prominent historian suggests that Hispanics were so dependent on servant labor that the Emancipation Proclamation, which freed the slaves in 1863 and outlawed peonage in 1867, profoundly affected the Hispanic domestic scene.[14]

Indian slaves wove on their own looms and in Spanish workshops on treadle looms that produced the *sarape* (for wearing), the frazada (for bedding), and yardage in the form of *sabanilla* (for sheeting and clothing). The looms also produced *jerga,* a twill-weave fabric for floor covering and sacks, *sayal* (sack cloth), and *bayeta* and *bayetón* (fulled cloth).[15]

In 1822, one of Diego's sons, José Rafael, registered as a citizen of Potrero,[16] a placita downstream from Rio Chiquito on the Santa Cruz River. Interestingly, José Rafael married one of his father's Indian slaves, a woman by the name of Maria Paula Martinez, who was known as Pablita, and it was thought that the move to Potrero may have been instigated by a position the family took on the marriage.

Later known as a handsome man with high cheekbones and smiling eyes that pierced the soul, Concepción Trujillo, one of four sons of José Rafael, was born in 1822.[17] He grew up on the Plaza del Cerro, the main plaza in Chimayó, but by 1848 at the age of 25 he had returned to the family holdings in Rio Chiquito where he described himself as a farmer residenced at San Miguel El Grande del Rio Chiquito.[18]

Concepción and María Juana Antonia Ortega Trujillo, c. 1903.

"There weren't any fences; there were open fields," Auntie Mercedes Trujillo, age 92, recollects:

> Concepción and each of his three brothers had marked off the land that he wanted. They farmed in Rio Chiquito and never left. They had sheep—I don't know how many. In the spring they would shear them and then card the wool and spin a single ply, very fine, and then in the winter, they would weave the *jerga* or frazadas to keep themselves warm when the snow was one or two feet high.[19] They would go to the mountains and cut wood with an ax to make the looms. For weaving they had reeds made of wood.[20]

Mercedes alludes to a time before milled lumber and sawmills appeared in the territory in the 1850s and 1860s that contributed to the evolution of looms with smaller frames. Later imported over the Santa Fe Trail, metal reeds would affect the width of the woven piece and the method of production.[21]

Unlike his brother Anastacio Trujillo, who dodged conscription by climbing a tree to avoid Union recruiters, the adventurous Concepción became one of three men from Chimayó to fight in the Civil War. He also joined the U.S. Army to fight in the Indian Wars, thus earning for his wife a pension from the federal government.[22]

Concepción was a man of tradition, prosperous and self-possessed. John R. Trujillo still remembers him riding from Rio Chiquito on a burro down to the Plaza del Cerro, in one instance to witness and revise the burial of Marcelino Trujillo. Concepción informed the mourners in no uncertain terms that particular day that Marcelino had been put to rest backward: they must rearrange the direction of the deceased, whose head, according to custom, must point north.

In the early years of the twentieth century, Concepción would buy cowhides from which to fashion *teguas,* leather shoes similar to moccasins. Mercedes can see him now just as he was right before his death, still going through the motions of making tewas, rolling the thin strips of imaginary hide across his thigh to make the laces that bound the teguas together.[23]

One of Concepción's nine children,[24] Isidoro Trujillo, born in 1867, inherited the boundless energy of his peripatetic father, an energy that paralleled an era made increasingly complex in 1880 by the coming of the Denver and Rio Grande Western Railroad, which linked nearby Española to Denver and to Santa Fe. The railroad was a decidedly mixed blessing, especially for the weaving industry. Many late-nineteenth-century innovations in weaving—commercial dyes, imported commercial aniline-dyed Germantown yarns from Pennsylvania, and cotton "string" warp adopted by the Hispano and the Navajo to replace (and not satisfactorily) wool warp—were introduced by the iron horse.

To their credit, these new yarn products were used effectively and imaginatively in such textiles as the Trampas-Vallero blankets, desirable enough to encourage Isidoro to make the long journey over the Borrego Mesa to trade for them with sacks of chile he had grown at La Centinela, the Trujillo ranch.

The prevailing economy in the villages of Northern New Mexico until near the end of the century was a subsistence one, finally giving way to a market economy that forced villagers to range hundreds of miles for a job that paid them wages.

Isidoro and María Francisca (Francisquita) Ortega Trujillo, c. 1898.

Isidoro Trujillo became part of this new order of things. In 1892, when in an arranged marriage he wed his first cousin, the lovely María Francisca ("Francisquita") Ortega (from the Plaza del Cerro Ortegas), the couple set off immediately afterward for Durango, Colorado, where Isidoro worked assiduously for his first wages in a smelter until 1902. Children were soon on the way, three girls and three boys. Teresita was the firstborn (1899) followed by Fedelina (1900), Mercedes (1904), Antonio Máximo (1907), Jacobo (1911), and Rosinaldo, the youngest, born in 1918.

Isidoro, along with his six brothers and two sisters, had inherited equal shares of his father's property in Rio Chiquito and at Centinela, a placita just southwest of there. He purchased additional acreage in the fertile Centinela Valley from the estate of his deceased sister, Higinia. He also was invited by his brother-in-law to jointly apply for an *herencia* (allotment) of open state land in what was termed a *pequeña tenencia,* or small claim, on the condition that the land be

Isidoro Trujillo's impressive chile harvest strung into ristras for drying, c. 1943.

fenced. After cutting hundreds of fence posts, digging hundreds of postholes, and clearing many acres with the help of two mules, Isidoro decided that he had as much land as he could manage and encouraged his brother Encarnación to apply for the rest.

These holdings became the beginnings of Centinela Ranch, later referred to as simply "La Centinela," for which Isidoro bought apple trees and planted an orchard. A ditch that came to be called La Acequia de la Centinela was dug off the Acequia del Burro in Rio Chiquito to irrigate the property. In order to meet the demands of La Centinela, even the children devoted much of the summer to the cultivation of wheat, corn, alfalfa, chile, melons, and onions.

There is a faraway look in Mercedes's eyes as she settles into a rocking chair and remembers: "My Daddy was a good man, and always working. When I was still very young, before we built the house at La Centinela, I would come from Rio Chiquito to bring him dinner every day, but it was hard to get him because he was always busy working the fields."[25]

Isidoro owned cows and horses and later bought sheep from shepherds who watched the flocks at El Alto, a high flat mesa east and slightly north of the valley. Coyotes were fierce at the time, and Jacobo (or Jake, as he came to be called) herded the sheep off the broad mesa at four o'clock every afternoon and down into the corrals for safekeeping. Sunday afternoon was for horse racing at El Alto, where neighbors from Chimayó, Córdova, and the surrounding area would gather together to test the speed and endurance of their favorite horses.

Improving the land at La Centinela took a great deal of time and effort. In 1916 the family decided to build a house at the base of Cuchilla de la Centinela that looked out over the orchards and fields below. Each year a room was added by the principal builders: Francisquita, Mercedes, and her brother, Rosinaldo or Ross. To make the adobe bricks, Mercedes and her mother would dig into the nearby hill for the clay soil, which was then mixed with water and straw from the *llanito* (small field) near where the animals were stabled.

A constant companion to her parents, Mercedes was and still is a handsome woman with an astonishing energy about her that once captured the heart of many a suitor, though she never married. In the old days, her first loyalty was to the immediate family, but her generosity of spirit then extended to the community at large, where she often could be seen cooking for a wedding or a funeral, caring for the sick, or tending to everyone's children. She still lives life to the fullest, and her strong faith in God follows her like a shadow.

"We didn't have a mortuary," she remembers.

> When people died, as a service to the community, my Daddy used to make coffins in the garage. Uncle Victor Ortega had a store in Chimayó on the Plaza del Cerro which sold linen. You could buy twenty yards for a dollar. With this, we would wrap the bodies of the deceased. And to preserve them, Mother would put salt on their belly buttons, tie the joints and bind the bodies to keep them straight in the casket, and we would bury them quickly.

In 1920, Isidoro began taking the mail to Cundiyó, aided by Ross and Jake when they were old enough. For this, Mercedes recalls, he kept twenty horses:

> A man would come in a buggy from Santa Cruz on the way to Truchas, leaving a mailbag for my Daddy, who would take the mail on horseback, even in the winter, to Cundiyó. The Santa Cruz leg of the journey took all day, but my Daddy would complete his trip to Cundiyó in an hour and a half, leaving the bags at the side of the road so that the next deliveryman could pick them up.
>
> It was safe to leave the mail in this way as there were never any holdups or robberies. In the summer, people often slept outside, and the doors to their homes were always open.

Often assisted by the boys, Isidoro would shear the sheep in the spring (churro crossed with Rambouillet and merino) and spread the fleeces in the sun to melt off the grease. It was the children's task to open the fleeces and card the wool whenever they had a chance.[26] During the winter, Isidoro also would card, and Francisquita, an excellent spinner until she went blind in 1953, would spin, afterward rolling the *lana* into big balls and then into skeins to wash with *amole* (yucca root), dye, and finally store in the attic for weaving in the winter.

The children learned about weaving at an early age from their parents, who took them to gather plant materials for dyeing—wild rose hips, *cañaigra* (sour dock), *chamiso,* sage, juniper, peach leaves, *tunas* (prickly pear fruit), and aspen bark from the nearby mountains.

One incident in particular not only encouraged young Jake to later excel at weaving but also focused the family on the potential financial rewards of their handspun, handwoven, and hand-dyed textiles. As Jake told the story:

> One day I was bringing the flock down from El Alto and there in the arroyo by our place were three couples having a picnic. They asked me what I was doing and I replied in halting English that I was taking care of my father's sheep. They asked me about the sheep, the wool, carding and spinning. When I said that my family was involved in every process, they asked, "Could we see some of the work that you people do?"
>
> I took them over to the house, and Mother started showing them blankets, both frazadas and sarapes, from the blanket chests. The youngest couple were newlyweds from Michigan and the others were in-laws. They started putting weavings aside and before I knew it, they had selected six.
>
> They told me to ask Mother how much she would take for them and she said $65 each. In those days $65 was an enormous amount of money for us, but the buyers were hardly fazed. This was my first sale and it really encouraged me to get started in weaving.[27]

THE PICNICKING VISITORS that Jake encountered exemplify one aspect of the Arts and Crafts Movement, a transatlantic movement that had started in England at the mid-nineteenth century. Thirty years later, enthusiastic visitors to the American Southwest began to perceive the crafts of the Native American—and, by extension, the native Hispanic—as indigenous and thus epitomizing American Arts and Crafts. In this way, first Navajo and later Hispanic textiles became curios for tourist consumption, with curio traders, who later evolved into blanket dealers, molding the work of weavers to Anglo tastes. "Native artifacts became part of Victorian-era home decorating, . . . and were incorporated into 'curio corners' for display"[28] in Victorian living rooms.

The phenomenon began in the New Mexico Territory in the 1870s when the first "specialist in the curio line," Jake Gold, the son of Louis (or Luis) Gold, proprietor of an early Santa Fe merchandising business, began to buy Indian goods from the nearby pueblos.[29] In about 1881, succeeding his brother in the family trade, Jake Gold opened Gold's Free Museum and Old Curiosity Shop.[30] Through this enterprise, he acted as liaison to the many crafts artisans, both Native American and Hispanic, who hoped to sell their wares to tourists. In 1889, he also published a catalogue of wholesale and retail goods that he offered to the Anglo markets.

Prototypical Chimayó, c. 1905, weaver unknown. Commercial 4-ply weft and 4-ply cotton warp, 36 x 76 inches.

The catalogue included pottery, equestrian equipment, mounted tarantulas and lizards, archaeological relics, and other eccentricities that one could purchase in collections priced from $1 to $50. The higher-priced collections contained woven blankets either from Mexico or Northern New Mexico supplied to Gold by itinerant merchants or peddlers who roamed the territory and were "a conduit for yarn or wool in one direction, blankets in the other."[31]

A second contributing factor to the enthusiasm for indigenous arts and crafts was the Tertio-Millennial Exposition held in Santa Fe in the summer of 1883. This "six week tri-cultural extravaganza celebrating the 333rd anniversary of Europeans on New Mexican soil" was a major tourist attraction.[32] One historian notes that "thousands of tourists visited Santa Fe at this time, and the substantial beginnings of the interest of travelers in Santa Fe and its many attractions date from this period."[33]

It was probably Jake Gold who developed "the simplified, tourist-oriented design styles in weaving that appear before the turn of the century"[34] and who thus was instrumental in modifying textile forms to accommodate the Arts and Crafts–inspired interior decorating fever that had settled over the Southwest.

In 1901, Jake Gold was recruited to run a store for Jesús ("Sito") Candelario, the son of a successful merchant family in Santa Fe.[35] Specifically, during Gold's tenure with Candelario, "the conga, or small sarape, . . . [was] transformed into the furniture scarf and pillow top."[36] Gold also developed "standardized sizes in weaving,"[37] an adaptation he promoted to make it easier and cheaper for the tourist and mail-order customer to consume these indigenous textile goods. He can even be credited with adopting the term "Chimayó" for a blanket style that evolved during this period.[38] The Chimayó-style blanket is discussed in depth in the later essay "Origins and Design Systems of Rio Grande Weaving."

Chimayó congita, c. 1920, weaver unknown. Commercial 4-ply weft and cotton warp, 20 x 20 inches. This piece has a red, black, and white coloration and design typical of early Chimayós woven for Sito Candelario by the Trujillo family.

Sito Candelario was no less a character than the colorful Jake Gold and stepped adroitly into Gold's shoes at his demise by creating local legends guaranteed to entertain any tourist and by collecting a menagerie of even more unforgettable curiosities than Jake Gold's, such as one large glass case of several human skulls![39] Candelario developed a thriving mail-order business and was in contact with such Navajo rug traders as J. L. Hubbell, C. N. Cotton, and C. and H. Algert, selling "Navajo weavings alongside Hispanic ones."[40]

Trading with other curio dealers in the Southwest and throughout the country, his business flourished in the first decade of the century, and by 1914 he was consigning several hundred shipments monthly.[41] He also advertised his curios in national magazines of the day and offered "curio corners" packaged as samplers of his collection for "a mere $10.00."[42] A typical offering was shipped in a barrel and included no less than twenty assorted pieces from different tribes . . . two pillow tops (Chimayó) . . . one Navajo loom . . . one Chimayó scarf. . . .[43]

Candelario tried out a variety of yarns from new yarn companies and sometimes compromised the quality of the textiles produced by "putting out" low-cost yarn to his Hispanic weavers, who would later regard him as "tight." But in 1906, he began to buy a smooth, four-ply yarn from J. & H. Clasgens Company of New Richmond, Ohio, which is still a popular supplier for New Mexican weavers today.

Mercedes is rocking in her favorite chair. Her eyes are focused on the distant horizon—perhaps it is La Mesa de las Viejas that she seeks—and they narrow as she begins to talk:

> I first began to weave for Sito Candelario in 1919 when I was only seventeen years old. One day, he came on horseback looking for weavers. Mother wove for him too and for E. D. Trujillo until her eyes started going bad.
>
> The blanket dealers would come from Santa Fe in wagons and bring us yarn, and we would weave. They sold small weavings and would buy ours, and they would also take our blankets to sell, or we would go to Santa Fe by wagon to

take the blankets in, rising early at four in the morning, arriving in Santa Fe by three in the afternoon. They would pay us very little, but it was better than nothing at all.[44]

Members of the Chimayó community could hardly fail to notice the enormous success of Sito Candelario and an Anglo named Julius Gans, who had also opened a shop in Santa Fe that sold blankets and jewelry. In surveying their few employment opportunities, some Chimayosos decided to try their own hand at being blanket dealers. According to Mercedes:

> Reyes Ortega was the first. He met an Anglo from whom he bought commercial wool, and he opened a shop and then put out a sign that read "Weaving Manufacturing." Then Uncle Nicasio Ortega started weaving using commercial yarn with a cotton warp, and he began to sell. Nicasio later bought wool warp, and after Severo showed him how, he wove with that.[45]

Ross Trujillo, Mercedes's youngest brother, who later grew to be over six feet tall, strong, self-sufficient, and decidedly a maverick, was only school-age at the time. He would pass on the way to lunch between the houses of Reyes and Nicasio Ortega, who lived next door to each other. Ross chuckles just to think about it:

> Uncle Nicasio was so competitive, if he saw a car drive up to his brother's, he would fly out his own front door first trying to lure the tourist away even before Reyes could greet him. This, of course, would be the end of Uncle Reyes' potential sale.[46]

In a community such as Chimayó where kinship ties and reciprocity had been the way of life for hundreds of years, the entrepreneurial spirit evident among the blanket dealers in the early twentieth century met with mixed response. Depending on the circumstances, blanket dealers could be nurturing or out for themselves or both.

Severo Jaramillo, a Chimayoso of Ortega descent, perfectly exemplified this. With no option but to work in the mines in Durango, Colorado, Severo worked sixteen-hour shifts for ten years to save enough to be able to open a business of his own. In 1918, he married Isidoro Trujillo's firstborn child and oldest daughter, Teresita, and in the process stepped easily into the role of *patrón* by accepting the responsibility of stewardship for his immediate and extended family.

He continued to work in the mines for an additional year, sending money home to his wife, but the work almost killed him, and soon he was forced to leave the mines for good. Afterward, as one of his grandsons, Tim Cordova, relates:

> Severo considered buying a ranch in Dolores, Colorado, but Teresita discouraged him saying she preferred for them to weave and garden in Chimayó instead. Then Severo decided to buy a motel and again Teresita said, no, she didn't want to wash sheets but preferred to weave and tend a garden in Chimayó instead.[47]

In 1919, a year after their marriage, and this time with Teresita's permission, Severo opened a small mercantile store in Chimayó. Teresita could finally weave and garden in the town she loved best. But the family income still needed supplementing so the two newlyweds and other members of the Trujillo family decided to weave for Julius Gans in Santa Fe.[48]

Severo, Helen, and Teresita Jaramillo posing with their car, c. 1932. The transportation afforded by a car opened up many markets to blanket dealers that would have been otherwise inaccessible.

Weaving was a discouraging proposition in those days, in part because the cotton string warp used in the looms would frequently break and the looms would then need readjusting. At Gans's suggestion, Severo decided to weave under the direction of master weaver Antonio Mier, who had recently arrived from Mexico to weave at the Gans shop. Mier soon pointed out to Severo that it was not the weaving that needed improving but the loom and warp that needed modification.

Severo Jaramillo with a customer in front of his shop in Chimayó, c. 1938.

From Mier, Severo learned how to build a better loom and how to warp with wool, a much stronger and thus superior fiber to the cotton warp that was being used in Chimayó. After leaving Mier's instruction, Severo took his knowledge of looms and warping to the community and then to the outlying regions such as Rio Chiquito, Cundiyó, Córdova, and Truchas, thereby helping to upgrade the weaving industry in Northern New Mexico.

When he decided to open his own weaving shop, Severo enlisted many of the weavers whom he had taught.[49] First he had a business upstairs in his home, but in 1938 he built a *comercio* that he called El Estación and from which he sold weaving, pottery, jewelry, and gasoline. A jaunty sign announced:

SEE A WEAVER MAKING BLANKETS
SEVERO JARAMILLO, TRADING POST

Before long, according to Ross:

> E. D. Trujillo, Eugenio Martinez, Ursulo Ortiz, Nicasio Ortega, Reyes Ortega, Lorenzo Trujillo—everybody—had a shop, and it was very competitive. Ursulo Ortiz would go to Gallup to undersell Severo Jaramillo. E. D. Trujillo would go to El Paso to undersell Ursulo. Severo would go to Phoenix or Denver and try to undersell them all.[50]

Ross accompanied Severo on many long business trips where he soon learned the test of family loyalty. On a dirt road all the way, it took a week and a half to drive to El Paso in Severo's open convertible —the backseat loaded up with suitcases full of blankets. And Severo made numerous stops in Albuquerque or Socorro or even Santo Domingo. Ross's job was to stay in the car and watch the blankets at all costs, and he soon learned that meant all day. Severo would finally return from one lengthy negotiation or another and off they would go again down the endless dirt road until late into the night.[51]

It is true that the blanket dealers provided income for Chimayosos at a time when there was little else to sustain them, but the profit that they realized on each and every woven textile was substantial. The blanket dealer succeeded according to the volume he sold. With pillow tops, orders for a hundred at a time were not uncommon. "On such an order, Candelario would make a profit of $.50 per pillow top or $50.00 on an order of 100."[52]

The Tewa Basin Report, which made a careful study of economic life in Northern New Mexico during the WPA years, corroborates the accuracy of these figures: "Only 10 percent of [vocational students involved in arts and crafts] will follow up and attempt to make a living at weaving or woodwork. The reason for this is that the wages per hour on handicraft work remain extremely low, 15 cents at best."[53] These figures were adjusted even lower by Ernest Lyckman, a state handi-crafts specialist under Brice Sewell, state director for vocational education and training. Lyckman suggested that a weaver could earn only ten cents an hour and commented that "The economics of it were absurd."[54]

According to a price-fixing agreement that was signed by E. D. Trujillo, Lorenzo Trujillo, Nicasio Ortega, Reyes Ortega, Severo Jaramillo, Ursulo Ortiz, Eugenio Martinez, and N. T. Martinez on December 6, 1929, Chimayó weavers were prohibited from negotiating a better deal for themselves. The agreement, which dictated the fixed prices weavers would pay for wool, wool warp, and cotton warp, also dictated the prices dealers would pay weavers for woven textiles of dimensions from 15 x 30 inches to 54 x 84 inches. The agreement even spelled out the design size for each size textile and the specified weight of finished material and included the following caveat:

> This work ought to be first class only and in order to achieve this, if need be the organization will lower its percentage. Whatever a worker sells in the way of wool, he must record with the patron; otherwise, he will be prohibited from working for anyone.[55]

It could be said that dealers took care of their own, as in the case of Severo Jaramillo, and while one person might argue that the dealers cooperated with each other, another might point out that their cooperative spirit, as attested to by the price-fixing agreement, was only to ensure a profit for themselves. Some dealers, such as Ursulo Ortiz, had a cadre of loyal weavers behind them throughout careers that spanned half a century. In later years weavers were known to leave long-time employment with dealers for a financial incentive in the 1970s of as low as ten cents per textile, a factor that tends to indicate how fragile their loyalties actually were.[56]

Interestingly, in spite of these facts and figures, many Chimayó blanket dealers are remembered by Chimayosos today with great respect and fondness, especially by the *viejitos,* or elders, of the community who worked for them personally. Not only are the early dealers perceived as having helped the community through such major economic crises as the Great Depression, they also are seen as having shepherded the community at large through the complex transition from barter system to market economy. Finally, there remains a special civic pride for the blanket dealer who achieved financial success and prestige within the community and who also could be regarded as successful in the larger and more cosmopolitan world beyond Chimayó.

It wasn't that weaving was "high stakes" in Chimayó but rather that it was the only game in town—a factor that sometimes enticed even villains. In a suspicious set of circumstances surrounding the disappearance of 120 pounds of handspun, hand-dyed wool, Isidoro and Francisquita's home—the bedrooms finally all built and a new tin roof installed over the garage and paid for with the money Mercedes had earned from weaving—burned to the ground one very cold night in the winter of 1928.

"At first," Mercedes remembers, "the family carried water in buckets from the ditch to put out the fire, but the water had turned to ice by the time they got to the house."

> Trembling and shaking, Mother threw on her new cape and went screaming toward the arroyo "We are burning! We are burning!" because she heard a car coming. Severo called out to her, "Come here, come here. You are going to go crazy."

The scene turned frantic:

> Teresita and cousin Marcelino were trying to dig the windows and frames out of the wall so they could save them from burning, but Severo was yelling, "No, no. Come over here and help us instead."
>
> Stored in the rafters were about 120 pounds of handspun, hand-dyed wool—enough for weaving twelve blankets. There was also meat drying in the rafters, sacks of sugar that Father had purchased with ristras of chile, and potatoes stored in a hamper.
>
> Jacobo ran all the way to cousin Mariano's in Rio Chiquito for help. "We are burning, we are burning," he said. Mariano cried, "Muchachos, muchachos, the world is burning!" His family got up and saw all the smoke here which was just thick because the wood was *ocote* [sapwood], so they came quickly, their buckets filled with dirt, not water, and helped to put out the fire.
>
> Afterwards, we didn't find anything except for the sugar which had melted into a blob and my Daddy's new hats he had taken from a closet and thrown up on the hill behind the house so they wouldn't burn. Most of the house except for the part that was roofed with dirt burned completely. Later, we spent a lot of time re-plastering to get rid of the soot. We built a new floor and tried to straighten the walls which had collapsed from the fire. Of course, Severo was there to help us.
>
> Later on, there were people farther down in Chimayó selling blankets of handspun wool and we knew it was our wool that had been stolen from our rafters before the fire was set to cover the theft. If the wool hadn't been taken, it would have melted into a puddle of grease and lanolin from the fire, but there wasn't a trace of it.
>
> We knew, in fact, who had done it, but we could prove nothing. He had passed through the arroyo when we were washing and dyeing the wool one day, all the wool for that winter, all 120 pounds of it, and the yarn spread out everywhere to dry.[57]

Jake Trujillo as a young man on horseback.

Second to the youngest in the Trujillo family was Jake, a gentle boy, delicate and beautiful to look at but solid and dependable to the core with a quiet presence and a way of affirming you that needed no articulation. He was masculine in his devotion to *el terreno,* the native land, which manifested in an ongoing dialogue with Centinela Ranch, but feminine in his attention to beauty. Even his humor was gentle and, bubbling up inside of him, would only occasionally overflow with a mirthful abandon that intoxicated everyone around. Plus, there was that way he had of flinging his head back to keep his thick brown hair out of his eyes.

An avid player in the drama of life, Jake could be a ham in front of the camera or when tourists were watching. He was a fine dancer, too, with a buoyant musicality that would erupt into song and cause women to fall in love with him more than they'd ever admit, but his shyness and his loyalty to the family always got in the way of a serious liaison.

Jake began weaving at the age of fourteen on a 20-inch loom that belonged to Sito Candelario. He wove the traditional handspun and hand-dyed frazadas, simple striped weavings of handspun yarn that he varied with bands of differing color. He also wove jerga on a four-harness loom in designs of herringbone, twill, and *ojo de perdiz* (partridge eye), whose patterning was controlled by a variation of the foot pedal work. He learned how to weave the twill used in jerga from working in the weaving shops of Preston McCrossen, who hired weavers to craft necktie material, and Julius Gans, where over the course of a year Jake became an expert at fly-shuttle work. "Jake was really proud," Irvin remembers, "because he could weave 35 yards of 36-inch fly-shuttle material in a day, which was then used to make ties."[58]

At age sixteen, Jake decided he needed a larger loom. He built a replica of the 54-inch loom that belonged to his brother-in-law Severo—a two-harness, four-pedal, traditional standing loom—and acquired his first experience weaving large "Chimayós" for Severo, who, by this time, had become a prosperous blanket dealer. Jake would later became famous for weaving the Chimayó blanket, a hybrid child of the Arts and Crafts Movement whose design, conceived near the end of the nineteenth century, would evolve throughout most of the twentieth.

One day in 1935, a representative of Charles Ilfeld and Company, a successful chain of mercantile stores in New Mexico and a seller of Chimayó weavings, asked Severo Jaramillo to find two weavers who could teach the Zuni Indians, situated some twenty-five miles from Gallup, how to use the floor loom. "Severo came in his car to the bachelor quarters by the barn where Jake and I were weaving," Ross remembered, "intending to enlist us for this assignment, and we were thrilled. We packed up our suitcases and hitched a ride to Santa Fe."

> Charles Ilfeld would even pay our transportation, so we bought our tickets at the train station in town and traveled on a bus to Lamy where we boarded the train for Gallup. For us, this was like going to the other end of the earth. When we arrived there, we were told to go to the lumber store and buy wood to make the looms, a bit of a surprise to us, but Charles Ilfeld & Company loaned us a Plymouth Suburban which more than made up for the inconvenience of having to fashion looms.
>
> Neither Jake nor I knew how to drive, but we somehow managed the twenty-five or thirty miles to Zuni where the work began. We built a 20-inch loom and a 48-inch loom in two or three days and stayed there for two months teaching the Zunis how to weave. Upon completing this assignment, Ilfeld paid us $250 each, a lot of money in those days. But when we got back, Severo wanted half of my salary in commission. I never paid it to him; I don't know if Jake did or not.[59]

Outwardly, Jake followed the dictates of family politics, showing his loyalty and gratitude to Severo by weaving on consignment for him almost exclusively. But after Jake began teaching weaving during the WPA era, he adopted the opposite stance of the blanket dealers whose raison d'être was the tourist trade. Instead, Jake came to endorse Anglos such as Mary Austin whose dramatic comment on her own involvement in New Mexican arts and crafts—"I got up from my bed and set the revival of Spanish colonial arts in motion"[60]—indicated something of the fever of her crusade.

In 1925, joined by Frank Applegate, Austin started the Spanish Colonial Arts Society in part to revive the tradition of "pure" Spanish weaving that existed before the tourist phenomenon. Austin and Applegate were encouraging dealers and weavers to turn against the imported, aniline-dyed commercial yarns that had become available from Germantown, Pennsylvania, and New Richmond, Ohio, and the cotton "string" warp that Hispanos and Navajos had adopted since the 1880s and in addition to abandon "certain garish colors" selected by the blanket dealers. Austin promoted instead the image of traditional, handspun, and authentic.[61]

Jake's prepared lecture notes for a weaving class at the Española Vocational Department in September 1933 supported her position:

> There are many distinguished [persons who are] critical of the use of aniline dyes for the home woven fabrics of the Southwest. Among these are Mary Austin, Ruth Laughlin Barker, Professor B. H. Sewell, the late Frank Applegate and others. These authorities on the Spanish Colonial period have at times pointed out the following as advantages of natural dyes: softer colors, greater permanency, less harmful dye process, a silkier and softer resultant fabric, truer color, etc.[62]

Jake Trujillo's weaving class at Española High School, 1933.

In 1932, Jake began teaching in a WPA-sponsored program at the University of New Mexico called the San Jose Training School Project. Here he instructed teachers in what he called the "basics" of weaving, including the spinning and dyeing of yarn.[63] Jake taught not only for the state but also at Española High School (1933-34), and at the Spanish Normal School at El Rito (1935-36).

"During the Depression years, weaving was almost dead," he later reminisced. "Very few of the old-timers were weaving."

> I built a small loom that would fit in a trailer and I would go out to the different communities south and west of Albuquerque like Socorro, Belen, Mountainair and Zuni and give lectures and weaving demonstrations to high school students in their regular assemblies. That's one way that we started reviving the art of weaving in New Mexico. I'm very proud that I played a part in . . . it.[64]

During this time Jake formulated a design theory whose principles he taught to students and which he practiced throughout his life: "Design must be true form and must follow function to beautify a given space. Design must have orderly arrangement and repetition of line as well as color."[65] He kept meticulous notes on the principles of weaving, many carefully detailed weaving orders for his students, and records of student supplies purchased from Native Market.

His students learned every aspect of weaving, from threading and setting up the loom to the different applications of materials, including carding, spinning, and hand-dyeing yarn with dyes made from plant materials. As a result, many students became young professionals whose textiles were consigned to leading retailers such as Nicasio Ortega and Leonora Curtain, who owned and subsidized Native

Market, a commercial scheme to sell native arts and crafts, which opened in 1933.

Jake's unmistakable and somewhat grave formality in the classroom was tempered by a genuine concern for his students that permeated the short, handwritten speeches he delivered to them at important times during the school year:

> Just a word or two to express my most sincere and kind feelings toward you. May you grow up as sweet as you look today and strive always for the best things this world possesses.[66]

And from time to time he gave short addresses on one aspect or another of the weaving profession:

> Spinning is the art of drawing, twisting and combining either animal or vegetable fibers so that they are formed into continuous thread for further operation of weaving, knitting and sewing.[67]

It also appears that during this time Jake considered writing his own book on weaving, a project that, regrettably, he never saw to fruition.[68]

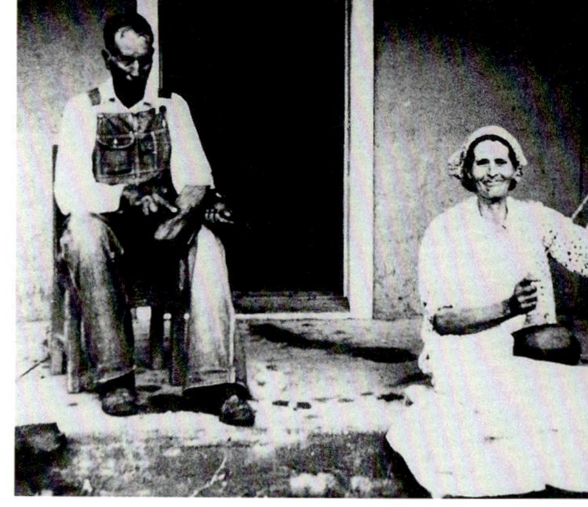

Isidoro and Francisquita Trujillo spinning under their portal, c. 1940.

His detailed records of weaving for his brother-in-law, Severo Jaramillo, indicate something of a business relationship that was handled with care. He kept track to the ounce of the yarn advanced to him, paid for it as soon as he could, carefully described the textile that he sent back for Severo to sell, and reweighed and recorded the yarn that was left over, a procedure that is still followed today between weavers and dealers.

For special orders there were elaborate annotations, measurements, and drawings. As each order was completed, he would write "PAID" across the transaction. From time to time he borrowed or advanced yarn to his brother Ross. He kept transaction records for Mercedes and Isidoro as well.[69]

JAKE SLOWLY PULLED AWAY from the painful anonymity and obscurity reserved for weavers by merchants, blanket dealers, and tourists. Beginning in 1939, weaving orders began to arrive from clients as far away as Bennington, Vermont; Boulder City, Nevada; Covington, Louisiana; and Denver. By 1941, his clients hailed even from Park Avenue in New York City.

In 1942, he joined the U.S. Navy, where he was originally assigned as a gunner on a merchant ship with duty in both the Pacific and the Atlantic theaters. In 1943, he was reassigned as an instructor of arts and crafts in a rehabilitation program on Treasure Island just outside of San Francisco where he taught leather tooling, tinwork, woodwork, spinning, and weaving.

It was during this time that Jake became reacquainted with a young woman he had met years before while teaching weaving at Española High School. She was delicate and feminine, her features as finely drawn as those of a china doll, and her name was Isabelle Garcia.

He returned from the war with his lovely young bride and a determination to escape the limited economic opportunities of Chimayó. Of course, the Trujillos would keep La Centinela, but during the week, they would live and work in Los Alamos, where, over the next thirty years, both were employed. Yet the City on the Hill was only a means to an end. For Jake Trujillo the end was economic freedom to pursue his lifelong passion for weaving.

Ironically, neither the blanket dealers who had encouraged the weaving of tourist curio textiles nor the wealthy Anglo patrons who had encouraged a return to a pure and traditional craft were completely successful in achieving their goals. Though native crafts were exhibited in the first Spanish Market in Santa Fe in 1926, the Spanish Colonial Arts Society that Mary Austin had helped to found neither supported nor encouraged Chimayó-style weavings because they were not comprised of handspun wool and hand-dyed yarn.

That organization, first active in the years between 1925 and 1934, was only partly successful in elevating the taste of New Mexicans in regard to both traditional weaving and the quality of weaving in the state. Following the deaths of Frank Applegate (1931) and Mary Austin (1934), the Spanish Colonial Arts Society temporarily closed its doors for lack of leadership. Other arts and crafts shops opened briefly and struggled unsuccessfully to survive. While Chimayó-style weavings continued to be ignored at these "native" shops because of their lack of "traditional purity," the textiles of many of Jake Trujillo's student weavers from vocational schools such as El Rito Normal School found amazingly receptive buyers.

In spite of the enthusiasm of wealthy Anglo patrons, by 1939 Hispanic crafts still had not achieved the financial and artistic status that Indian crafts (now deemed "art") enjoyed. However, when World War II broke out, it no longer seemed to matter. Both weavers and nonweavers abandoned their peacetime occupations in favor of the war effort.

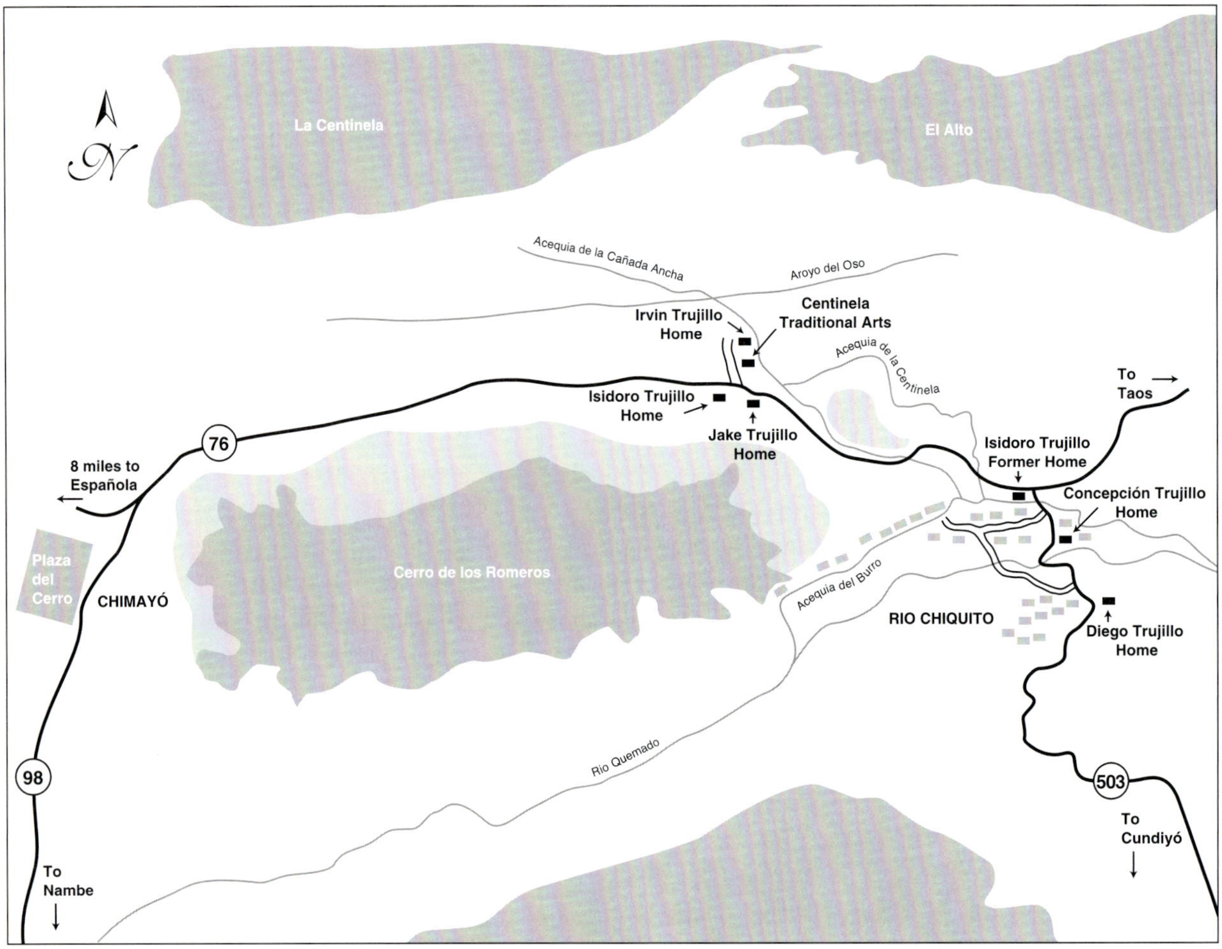

La Centinela
El Alto
N
Acequia de la Cañada Ancha
Aroyo del Oso
Irvin Trujillo Home
Centinela Traditional Arts
Acequia de la Centinela
To Taos →
Isidoro Trujillo Home
Jake Trujillo Home
76
8 miles to Española ←
Isidoro Trujillo Former Home
Concepción Trujillo Home
Plaza del Cerro
CHIMAYÓ
Cerro de los Romeros
Acequia del Burro
RIO CHIQUITO
Diego Trujillo Home
Rio Quemado
98
503
To Cundiyó ↓
To Nambe ↓

Centinela Traditional Arts viewed from the south

INTO THE PRESENT

La acequia de la Cañada Ancha, the Centinela irrigation ditch, extends west beyond Irvin Trujillo's property, which today consists of an adobe house, barn, sheds, and the studio and shop of Centinela Traditional Arts. The houses of his immediate family occupy the middle and south sections of the valley.

The land is covered with snakeweed, prickly pear cactus, chamisa, and juniper, all used for dyeing the churro wool spun by Trujillo weavers for centuries. As one ascends the north ridge, fields of alfalfa, chile, and apples spread out on either side of the valley. To the north, on the other side of the ridge, the Badlands retreat into the distance. Somewhere in that direction, under a nice outcropping of cottonwoods and a spring, is La Mesa de las Viejas, where, according to Auntie Mercedes Trujillo, the crazy people always go.

Our gaze is directed across the south valley to a road built in 1920 that cuts through the Centinela incline and that, in 1945, became a conduit to Los Alamos, the Atomic City that provided jobs for the few Chimayosos enterprising enough to engage in the bustling activity of the postwar era. Here in this peaceful valley, somewhere between the past and the future, between tradition and invention, between the old and the new (in a paradigm of contradictions), Irvin was born to Jacobo and Isabelle Trujillo in 1954.

It wasn't that Irvin's parents wanted to live and work in the Atomic City or that Jacobo's wartime career in the U.S. Navy had somehow catapulted him into the complex defense stratagems that would finally end the Second World War. It was that earning a good living in Chimayó was no longer economically feasible, a reality driven home by the failed federal agricultural projects of the New Deal in New Mexico.[70] So the Trujillos and others like them lucky enough to find work elsewhere became part of a significant exodus of people from the pristine Northern New Mexico villages that could no longer sustain them.

Every Sunday night after the supper dishes were cleared and the ranch matters settled for the week, they said goodbye to Grandmother Francisquita and Auntie Mercedes in Chimayó, where they had spent the weekend, backed their automobile loaded with produce from the ranch slowly out of the driveway, and headed west toward Española. Then they proceeded along the infamous stretch of road once known as the "Roller Coaster" because of its dizzying configuration as it crossed the Rio Grande River and began its winding and precarious ascent along the face of the Jemez Mountains where mesas formed tremendous bluffs and canyons rose almost 7,500 feet above sea level. Carved directly out of the rocky cliff, the road circled the top of Los

Alamos mesa and suddenly streamed onto the tableland at one of only two gates in the nine-foot-high, double barbed wire fence that surrounded the entire city.[71]

A permanent resident—his security pass approved by the FBI—Irvin Trujillo's father could come and go as he pleased, but many years after the war, Los Alamos still remained as closely guarded as any community in the world. Whether it was the imposing gates at both entrances, the Security Service Guards in trooper hats and gray-blue uniforms that clustered around them, the guard towers above the gates manned day and night, or the two tanks commanding the road on either side, you knew you were in an alien place.[72] Even as the mesas were patrolled by the Los Alamos Mounted Police, K9 Corps dogs guarded the canyons below.[73]

It had not gone unnoticed that the City of Bombs would be a prime target in any war. When President Harry S. Truman concluded that "the Russians probably had pierced all our secrets through espionage," when Russia's Sputnik became the first man-made earth satellite and Senator Joseph McCarthy's methods of investigating communism were leaked to the press, paranoia became just another imposing presence in the town.[74] There were rumors among the Hispanic villages that "the Hill" produced spaceships, but Irvin's father knew that Los Alamos designed, instead, hundreds of weapons capable of unprecedented destruction, just a mile from his front door.[75]

Whether it was the treachery of the mountainous roads and threat of a traffic accident, thoughts of communism and espionage, or just the vague sense of foreboding caused by leaving a home like Francisquita's where you were loved, where Spanish was spoken, and where the only plumbing was the cold running water that came from a well nearby, Isabelle would always begin saying the rosary out loud just as the car turned west on State Road 76, and the others would follow.

For young Irvin Trujillo, Chimayó was a place of substance and meaning, a resort of simple pleasures: the indulgence of a 12-ounce Coke from Uncle Severo Jaramillo's Coke machine, the daily inspection of the field of chile and corn across the road, the dirt pile where he played with his cousins, or *primos*. And from Chimayó there were forays into richer pastures: trips to Española with its A&W Hamburgers, the J. & W. Owens Variety Store, or even Bond and Willard, a hardware emporium capable of satisfying a boy's most fantastic yearnings.

Pat and Irvin Trujillo in Los Alamos, c. 1956.

His parent's humble Los Alamos duplex was drab, even sterile, by comparison. Its efficient and utilitarian design was serviceable for adults but boring and lifeless for a child with Irvin's imagination, and besides, there were no primos to play with. Jake would occasionally remind the children that they were seventh-generation Trujillos, an entitlement that seemed somehow irrelevant, as he rarely had time to play with them and seldom talked about the past. However, when the now famous Northern New Mexican establishment, Rancho de

Chimayó, opened its doors in 1965 and Irvin's older sister Pat spent the following summer in Chimayó in order to work there, Jake set up a giant 6 x 7–foot loom in her vacant bedroom, which, in due time, came to dominate the entire domestic scene.

Irvin was fascinated. The loom made an awful racket, but every night after dinner, he could hear his father singing above it in Spanish the old romantic tunes of his youth. At the end of each night, Jacobo would move the spools of thread and uncover the design that had been shielded by a cloth protector as the evening's work progressed. After a couple of weeks, Irvin asked if he could help and soon found himself standing on a chair at the side of the loom moving the spools of yarn needed for the design. He was ten years old and elated to become part of such a mysterious pastime. Soon Jake heard a plaintive request: "Get me a loom, Dad, I think I can do it."

Within a week Irvin had his own loom and was learning from his father about threading, tying the warp, and throwing the shuttle. Then came instructions in shuttle technique: *paladar* (pick and pick) and beading. Soon, weaving was a bond between them—something a reticent man and a shy young boy could actually talk about.

"When the weaving was perfectly aligned on the loom, the beater made a solid 'poom'," Irvin recalled,

> as it packed the woven threads. I had been playing drums for two years by then and the rhythm of the drums and the rhythm of the beater soon began to harmonize in my imagination.

The child was proud of his first weaving, a small, striped rectangle with his sister's initials in the center. He showed it to his best friends, who wanted monogrammed weavings for themselves. Jake suggested how much to charge and Irvin soon began taking his first weaving orders.

Within months he was weaving for the Ortegas, another family of weavers with a shop in Chimayó, mostly 20 x 20–inch squares for tourist consumption. He wove ten of them a day and would deliver a stack each week, surveying what he had left the previous week to see if any remained. But by the end of the summer, after calculating his wage at ninety cents an hour, Irvin was discouraged. Fortunately, in late August at a Los Alamos crafts fair, he sold all the additional pieces he had woven for $10 each, netting, to a child's way of thinking, a handsome profit:

> The second summer I worked for myself. I ended up raising chile another summer, but the cows got into it at harvesttime, so there was no chile and no profit. The next summer, I was back at the crafts fair selling my weavings again.

In high school, Irvin moved to a 36-inch loom and for a graduation present received from Jacobo a 54-inch loom with a reed, or comb, for packing the weft that had belonged to his grandfather, Isidoro, who had used it for handspun pieces with cotton warp. This was a definite tie to the past.

In 1972, Irvin entered Eastern New Mexico University in Portales to earn associate degrees in machine design and civil technology. The reward, however, was discouraging: a job at Sandia National Laboratory drafting in a high-security vault with no windows. Irvin hated it. Where was the brilliant, ambient light, the openness and fresh air of Chimayó where he had returned to weave over long Christmas vacations from college? In 1975, he entered the University of New Mexico (UNM) at Albuquerque to study civil engineering—a field he not only excelled in but one that would greatly color his later work in weaving—and graduated four years later.

In 1979, the Museum of International Folk Art in Santa Fe published the first comprehensive book on Rio Grande textiles—a volume that was illustrated with Saltillos and Valleros and Chimayó weavings discussed in the context of a revival that, it implied, had been instigated for the tourist market. Most significantly for Irvin the book explored the breadth of the Rio Grande weaving tradition, suggesting that its boundaries extended far beyond the familiar Chimayó-style weavings. It also demonstrated the diversity of design within aspects of the tradition, especially in the case of Saltillo sarapes. Irvin was both concerned that his people had been weaving some form of tourist art and inspired to know more about the past:

> In Chimayó, the guys spoke Spanish so I clearly wasn't one of them, but in Los Alamos my Spanish surname seemed foreign, so I wasn't one of them either. I was stuck somewhere in the middle. After Reies Tijerina's raid on the Rio Arriba County Courthouse which occurred when I was only thirteen, I became terrified of my Hispanic culture, a terror which certainly contributed to my growing identity crisis.

Weaving helped to ground Irvin, but learning about his heritage was even more rewarding. What followed was a gradual process of self-discovery:

> After reading the book on Rio Grande textiles and getting Dad to show me his WPA ledger books, I began to understand something of my father's origins, his work for the blanket dealers and the opposing values presented by the Spanish Colonial Arts Society and their efforts to promote and sell "pure" Hispanic textiles through Spanish Market. And I learned there was a lot more to my family than just being Spanish. They had enjoyed a long and distinguished weaving tradition from the earliest days in New Mexico.

In 1979, Nancy Murphy, a graduate of the University of Notre Dame, arrived to apprentice with Irvin's father. She also was interested in natural dyes and asked Irvin to join her in this additional pursuit. Out came Jake's WPA ledger books again, which also had dye recipes in them. But where did one get the ingredients? Irvin and Nancy began to gather sage, juniper, and chamisa and from a local pharmacy purchased cochineal, a red dye substance made from the ground carcasses of a species of beetle. The tiny matchbox-sized packages cost $20 each. Then they started their first mordant vat.[76]

Dyeing involved chemistry, not a discipline in which Irvin had excelled in college, but its practical applications soon became evident as he struggled to make dark red by adding rhubarb leaves for their oxalic acid to a cochineal dye bath. The recipes for dyeing seemed both random and scientific. He could achieve a rust color by using cañaigra root or plum root and adding black walnuts. Or, if he wanted to buy a European dyestuff, he could achieve brown tones by using catechu, or cutch, extract derived from the acacia bush.

Natural dyes allow for much subtler shadings within colors. There have been many synthetically dyed textiles that customers considered flawed because the color didn't match exactly, but with natural dyes, these "flaws" add to the aesthetic value of the textile and are called *ombré,* which is French for "shade."

One of the most significant contributions Centinela Traditional Arts has made to the weaving industry is the use of natural dyes and their application to a tradition of weaving that developed with commercial dyes. The Chimayó blanket, for example, and its strong coloring (aniline red, black, and white) and design had been based on commercial dyes transported from the East first over the Santa Fe Trail and later, after 1880, by rail. When Irvin decided to use natural dyes, the results were magnificent and much subtler in palette than the yarns available to other Chimayó weavers. Jake had always emphasized that color was the most important part of a textile. His early reputation as a colorist, and the color innovations that resulted from the natural dye experiments for which the Trujillos soon became famous, put them into a niche that very few Hispanic weavers occupied. In fact, few others were even dyeing their own wool.

In 1980, Irvin met Lisa Rockwood, in his words, "a beautiful woman with masses of brunette hair all the way to her hips." Lisa's childhood had lacked the continuity and stability that even Irvin's Janus-faced upbringing had enjoyed. Her father was a patent agent with an electrical engineering background who moved the family a great deal in the early years of his career.

When he was hired by Los Alamos National Laboratory, they relocated to New Mexico, and Lisa soon found herself in Irvin's former high school experiencing the same cold and impersonal atmosphere that Irvin recalled so vividly about the place. She had always excelled in crafts and needlework, and in Los Alamos these became her refuge. There she explored beadwork with heishi, needlework, and silversmithing. Later introduced to the loom, she was hardly intimidated by it.

Lisa entered UNM on scholarship and met Irvin her second year in college—April 7, 1980, to be exact. Irvin was playing in a rock band that year, which absorbed every moment of his free time. Each afternoon after work he would leave the U.S. Army Corps of Engineers and head for a practice session with his band, where he remained every night until ten:

> That Friday night there was a gig at UNM. We were playing rock and roll and I was on a lighted platform wearing a pair of turquoise spandex pants. I was putting away my drums after our performance, and this girl with the amazing hair that I had been watching all night came walking up and asked me if I knew a drummer who might play in her band.
>
> I wrote down her name and called her within the week. She was only a beginning guitarist, but how else could I get to know her? Besides, I thought it

might be interesting playing drums in an otherwise female band. Much later I learned I had reminded her of her teenage idol, Graham Gouldman, a British pop star and songwriter.

The practice sessions ended when summer did, but by then a romance between the two had begun.

Lisa had been grappling with a profession, and Irvin, inspired by his highly successful blanket-dealing uncle, Severo Jaramillo, confided his dream of creating a profitable weaving concern. A business plan Lisa wrote up for a class project also pointed to a successful Chimayó weaving venture. With all the Trujillos gathered in Jacobo's living room in the fall of 1981—Pat and husband Marco, Jake and Isabelle—Irvin and Lisa discussed their ambition: a seven-year goal in which to be weaving full-time.

Irvin had been talking marriage, and the two were wed the following May. Their honeymoon, a stay at La Fonda in Santa Fe, included a visit to the Wheelwright Museum, which was featuring an exhibition of Saltillos. Lisa now became doubly enamored: weaving Saltillos remains her specialty even today.

"My first connection to Lisa Rockwood was through music," Irvin recalls,

> but weaving became another bond between us. On such an ambitious scale, it was like diving into uncharted waters. I would have married Lisa even if she hadn't gotten into weaving, but I probably would never have gotten into it so deeply myself.

Jake, who in 1975 had retired from his job at Los Alamos and returned permanently to Chimayó to live, was busy with weaving commissions but offered to take care of customers if the youngsters helped open a shop. They could add on to his weaving room by including an adjacent shed and garage. And so the plan took shape. The garage doors were closed off, a carpet installed, and the walls painted; the shop opened in mid-July 1982.

THE PROBLEM WAS that Jake sold Lisa's first textiles, 20 x 20–inch pieces, as quickly as she could weave them, but she longed to weave more complex pieces that would take even more time to complete. When she decided to advertise for apprentice weavers in the college newspaper, surprisingly, many people responded. From an original pool of fifteen student weavers, several became very productive, and one, Danni Webb, still sells her magnificent version of the traditional Mexican *quechquemitl* shawl at Centinela today.

In 1985 Rudy Valdez, who had worked for Ortega's weaving shop, appeared at the door and asked if Lisa and Irvin could put him and his family to work. Rudy's welcome arrival relieved Centinela of much of the pressure from the demanding tourist business.

In 1987 Denise Miller, a graduate of the Rhode Island School of Design, arrived to ask if she could work and was immediately employed to help dye yarn. She later began to weave for Centinela and made an enormous contribution to the shop by teaching Irvin that he could never dictate design ideas to someone with a creative mind.

Spanish market had been initiated in 1926 to promote interest in and encourage native Hispanic crafts but had closed its doors in 1934 as had its sponsor, the Spanish Colonial Arts Society, for lack of support. In 1965 the market resumed its activities, first in affiliation with Indian Market, but then in a gesture of independence in 1971 it rearranged its market dates to host its own annual celebration around the Santa Fe Plaza and under the portal of the Palace of the Governors.

In 1977 the director of Spanish Market asked Jake if he would exhibit, and Jake in turn asked Irvin to join him. "He told me exactly what to weave," Irvin remembered, "a classic textile from the Rio Grande tradition—a piece with natural colors, just gray and white, with small chevrons in the center of a rosette design. To my surprise, the piece won second place!"

The following year, 1978, the modest first prize was given to a highly skilled female weaver, Teresa Archuleta Sagel, whose ultimate reward was her ability to subsequently sell her textiles for several thousand dollars apiece. Irvin went over to look at her work, "beautiful textiles with natural dyes. I decided then and there that I would just have to learn how to dye wool."

The third year Irvin exhibited at Spanish Market, he failed to win a prize in spite of his newly acquired natural-dyeing techniques. In fact, it was Jake who got a prize using yarn that Irvin and Nancy Murphy had dyed for him. Still, the Trujillos sold a number of textiles. This time Teresa Archuleta Sagel entered an ikat piece. "What was ikat?" Irvin wondered. "I was too proud to ask her how to do it."

Alan Vedder, the noted conservator of Spanish Colonial art, screened Lisa for Spanish Market in 1982, a year in which the whole family entered weavings and won first prize, second prize, and honorable mention, ending up on the front page of the *Santa Fe New Mexican*!

Lisa and Irvin Trujillo at Spanish Market, 1985.

Two years later, when Lisa entered an even finer weaving, the subject of her non-Hispanic background came up at the annual membership meeting. Though Jake defended her brilliantly by saying that she was part of his family—and Jake was by then at the hub of Spanish Market prestige—the issue of her origins was hotly debated. Finally, the board decided to "grandfather" her in. (She had, by that time, participated in Spanish Market for three years.)

While the society focused on the issue of Lisa's cultural heritage, the real question has not to this day been addressed. Do the Spanish Colonial Arts Society and other institutions that promote and collect Spanish Colonial art exist to support people of Hispanic heritage or the artistic expression of pure Spanish Colonial arts? Even today, though nationally collected by individuals, Lisa's textiles, which are traditionally Spanish Colonial in technique and in their design systems, are still not collected by institutions that promote Spanish Colonial arts.

"Spanish Market was both a traumatic and an exhilarating event for all of us," Lisa remembers. "It was simply the biggest deal in the world, the biggest deal in our family's lives." By 1986, Spanish Market competition had turned into a rivalry that was always intense between the top weavers. Even within the Trujillo family, according to Lisa, "the spirit of encouragement and competition was always followed by the consequence of winning or losing." Spanish Market proved to be an enormous incentive for achievement part of the year, but what happened the rest of the time? For Irvin, "Lisa and I became a team experimenting together and encouraging each other to compete against ourselves."

WHILE STILL RESIDING in Albuquerque, the younger Trujillos decided to design and build an adobe house on the Trujillo property in Chimayó specifically for dyeing and weaving—two sinks for rinsing, two stoves for dyeing, extremely low countertops, and an abundance of sunlit space for weaving at large looms. In fact, "the dye house" proved to be so charming that they chose to move from Albuquerque in December 1984 and live in it instead.

It was also time, in 1987, for them to build their own studio rather than depend on the good will of Jake, whose gallery, with its poor lighting and cramped space, they had endured for years. "My father's shop had a bare 60-watt light bulb in the middle of a very closed-in room," Irvin remembers. "I wove facing the wall under a ceiling that barely cleared my head and gave me a sense of suffocating claustrophobia."

The new Centinela Traditional Arts had eleven-foot ceilings with a pitched roof extending to fifteen feet. The walls were massive and made of adobe. There were skylights for a generous amount of natural lighting with Lisa's loom set up directly under one of them so that she could interact with the customers and weave at the same time. Irvin made a structure for track lighting to showcase the largest textiles and set wooden strips into the adobe walls from which to hang them. He also installed finishing tables. An abundance of rack space displayed all the naturally dyed colors that the studio had created. One textile for which a special lighting system had been designed was even suspended from the ceiling; many others mounted on the wall were displayed as art. The new environ was connected by a door to Jake's studio so that Lisa and Irvin could still interact with him, only on a somewhat more limited basis.

Irvin Trujillo at the loom in the new studio.

JAKE WAS FREE OF the turbulent years of blanket dealer dominion and the patronage of wealthy but equally controlling Anglo aesthetes, free to simply be himself, a master weaver of not only traditional "pure" Hispanic textiles—the handspun, hand-dyed, and handwoven Rio Grandes—but also of the Chimayó-style blanket, which he had helped to shape and evolve. His reputation first grew statewide, then nationally, and the ribbons and awards that he took from textile events were mostly blue and in ever-increasing numbers. Still, something seemed somehow out of place. Vaguely disquieting at first, it began to gain energy and momentum.

It wasn't the almost supernatural speed at which culture had reinvented itself through technology in the last quarter of the nineteenth and the first decades of the twentieth. The magnitude of those changes had quite literally altered man's view of the universe. No, the old should give way to the new. It was something about the family structure that had changed; that and leaving the simple life of the land for the complex one on "the Hill," which somehow had rearranged the value of things. Jake lived, after all, for others. It had always been so—as true in the case of Isidoro as it had been for Concepción or José Rafael or even old Diego. A man lived on the land and always for others and honored the family until he dropped dead in the fields or until he eased, in sleep, from the obligation of living such a life. Life was sacrifice; it was meant to be. Jesus had taught as much, and the Penitente Brotherhood, a local religious community of Catholic laity, reaffirmed the faith every year during Holy Week.

Isabelle, Jake, and Mercedes Trujillo at the Centinela fruit stand, 1980.

But somewhere, somehow into the very texture of things, the peace that should flood one's life near the end with abundance as nothing else ever would had somehow ebbed away. Perhaps it was the independence of his children, their sense of self-initiative and self-responsibility, their seeming disregard for the role of paterfamilias—this was the beginning of the conflict. Where was their faith? One should cherish but never question, respect but never challenge. One should protect the family's honor but never reveal the family's fragile truths.

Much of Jake's failing health may have been caused by this tremendous inner conflict. The old would never, could never concede to the new. As the days went by he felt more and more depleted. He contracted pneumonia after attending Winter Spanish Market in December 1989. Weak but recuperating, he then scheduled a trip to San Diego for a long-dreaded jaw operation, where doctors confided that he also had pancreatic cancer. Intent on keeping this from the family, Jake returned, seemingly improved at first, but he started to decline rapidly. By the early spring of 1990, he had reached the point where he could no longer operate his looms. He would go into his studio but just sit there looking out at the skeletal apple trees in the orchard. The Trujillos were featured in an exhibition at the Roswell Museum that March. Upon their return, Jake entered the hospital in Española and died within two weeks.

Irvin and his father had differed on many issues throughout their lives; conspicuously apparent was their opposed marketing approaches. The younger Trujillos always credited each weaver in the shop with his or her own work while Jake would acknowledge to customers that others wove for him but never revealed their names. His reasoning evolved, of course, from his own relationship with blanket dealers in the early days when he was neither paid sufficiently nor was given artistic credit for his work.

There had been many generations of weavers in the Trujillo family, but each had surpassed the one before. "Dad was really very proud that he had taken up his father's tradition and had excelled at what his father had done," Irvin mused. "Before he died, Dad was weaving pictorials; yet Isidoro had never even woven Chimayós. It was during my Dad's generation that the best of Hispanic weaving finally was elevated to art."

Lisa and Irvin have created a memorial to Jake in his former studio: a collection of archival photographs that offers visitors some background history on La Centinela and Chimayó weaving in the early twentieth century. One singular image of Jacobo as a very young man posed in a field with a spinning wheel—his arm elegantly suspended in midair, a sarape thrown capriciously over one shoulder, his brow slightly furrowed as he gazes away from the camera—dominates this tableau. Jake was an enormous inspiration to his son, who would otherwise never have taken up weaving as a full-time occupation.

Jake Trujillo at the wheel.

IRVIN TRUJILLO

"If I'm going to be a weaver, what am I going to weave?" Irvin wondered. "I wanted to weave textiles I'd never seen before, and in order to do this, I had to learn what had been done.

"I was afraid that the weaving tradition might have effaced itself, that the energy and inspiration generated from the classic pieces that had fueled the revival in the early years of the twentieth century might have dissipated, that there would be nothing to research. Fortunately, I was wrong.

"Lisa and I began with books. While there were ten to fifteen good volumes out on Navajo weaving, there was only one on Hispanic weaving at the time. And so we became sleuths: We visited the microfilm library in the basement of UNM, we visited the History Library at the Palace of the Governors, we poured over numerous issues of *El Palacio*. We examined a fabulous textile collection at the Laboratory of Anthropology that had rarely been seen in years; and in order to see some of the several thousand exceptional weavings at the Museum of International Folk Art, we even helped Nora Fisher change the paper which lined them.

"I decided in 1984 that I wanted to start weaving full-time and gave up my job at the Army Corps of Engineers that winter. Lisa was weaving double-wide blankets, which were selling for a good bit, so I felt that I could afford to quit working for others and work for myself.

"Ikat was, and still remains, a relentlessly fascinating subject. To date, approximately sixteen historic weft-faced ikat pieces have been found that are attributed to New Mexico. Ikat describes a resist-dyeing process in which warps and/or wefts are arranged according to pattern, then wrapped, bound, and dyed. The old ikat pieces were probably tied with cornhusks, just like making tamales. I use Japanese cellophane ikat tape. When the warps or wefts are dyed, the binding resists the dye and thus produces a patterned yarn that will create the desired design in the finished textile.

Irvin Trujillo holding the warp for a large custom jerga, 1994.

"Most of the classic ikat pieces contain only small geometric designs repeated over and over. Lisa and I wanted to expand on this and exper-

The Spider and the Hook, 1995, by Irvin Trujillo. Commercial 4-ply, natural-dyed weft with 2-ply warp, 54 x 84 inches. Collection of the National Museum of American Art, Smithsonian Institution.

Contains double-tied and -dyed figure ikat and most of the colors are overdyed yarn (yarn dyed in one vat of a color and then in a second color): indigo over chamisa, cutch over cochineal, and cutch over madder root, black walnut hulls, brazilwood, and chamisa.

imented with ikat in different ways: combining weft ikat with tapestry and using warp ikat as a vertical border in the warp with a central tapestry motif.

"Ikat is difficult in its own right, but by using engineering skills I could create designs that were more sophisticated technically than those of the average weaver who had little access to applied calculus. To enlarge an ikat design from a small drawing or cartoon, I had to use coordinates to compute the rise and run. I also expanded to figure ikat, by calculating the curves inherent in the design using calculus and a cartoon. And there was tapestry ikat, a concept that I communicated to Lisa, who created a diamond ikat piece, the first that I know of [see *Hyperactive,* page 50]. Both were ideas I hadn't seen explored before in weaving yet still derive from the Rio Grande tradition.

"I wanted to know what indigo meant; it wasn't just a dye. What was its history? How did it come to evolve? It didn't grow here but had to be imported from Mexico. Who brought it? Had the Hopi or the Navajo used it before the Spanish arrived, or were the Spanish the first to use indigo? I wanted our weaving tradition to be authentic. If the Spanish had introduced it to this region, I figured it was a legitimate part of our tradition.

"I used to put the Navajo on a pedestal because they were weaving all these fancy textiles, but they weren't weaving them before the Spanish got here. The Navajo had taken the idea of weaving and run with it, but they had not invented the craft. It was, after all, the Spanish who brought the first sheep here.

"I then began to research the Moki pattern ('Moki' was the old Spanish name for the Hopi) in which blankets were decorated with alternating panels of blue and brown (or black) stripes that were separated by stripes of white. That year, 1984, for the first time, in a process that began with *Moki Inspirado* [page 31], I created a narrative behind a textile—a dialogue, in fact. In this piece the Moki pattern makes up the background as well as the center of three converging diamonds. The diamonds represent the three cultures—Spanish, Pueblo, and Navajo—that managed to share the Moki pattern in spite of a history of struggle to coexist. Thus, *Moki Inspirado* reflected some of my thoughts on the nature of indigo—where it had come from and who brought it to New Mexico. *Moki Inspirado,* the result of this dialogue with myself, won the grand prize at Spanish Market in 1984, which really boosted my ego. This was also the first time that I had ever bested my father in a weaving competition.

"From my drafting experience as an engineer I also had learned about descriptive geometry, which enables one to look at an object from any plane at any angle and be able to draw it. I'd also studied isometrics and two- and three-point perspective drawing. For some of my designs, I actually render a drawing on graph paper and then draw coordinates figured out mathematically.

"I also have conducted experiments with Fibonacci, a process involving a graduated numerical sequence.[7] M. C. Escher, who created

Moki Inspirado, 1984, by Irvin Trujillo. Commercial worsted, single-ply, natural-dyed weft with 2-ply warp, 72 x 118 inches. Collection of Dorothy C. Haase.

the illusion of anthropomorphism with geometric forms, experimented with Fibonacci. I also have developed designs around the golden mean, and I have employed a French tapestry technique called *hachure,* or hatching, which uses line to create shading.

"An artist friend once told me my father was the first weaver he'd ever known who could create depth in a textile. Dad used color to achieve depth, not just surface design. My color studies developed from trying to understand how he accomplished this. I began these experiments in 1985 and included numerous shades of the same color to create tonality. I also experimented with outlining and using black and white to make neighboring colors advance or recede. When I'm weaving a textile that involves this approach, the process is very three-dimensional. I have found that my more recent pieces look best at about forty feet, so I think my approach may be working" [see *Figure with Shadow,* page 33].

"I AM FASCINATED with the technical aspects of weaving, not just the aesthetics. The loom is both the harbinger of the Industrial Revolution and the precursor of the computer age. But as far as I know, no industrial advances in weaving can match the aesthetic of a hand-woven piece. Look, for example, at a Pendleton blanket. There will be a positive image on one side of the blanket and a negative image on the other. The best industrial looms, even the Jacquard loom, cannot weave a tapestry with identical (right-sided) images on both sides, as in the Rio Grande tradition.

"The loom has evolved tremendously. The introduction of milled lumber, a major improvement over massive hand-hewn logs, changed and refined its structure. In New Mexico, an improvement equally as significant was the presence of the Bazán brothers, master weavers from Mexico City brought here in 1807 by the governor in Santa Fe to train young weavers in the area.

"Antonio Mier, another master weaver, who arrived in Santa Fe from Chihuahua in 1908,[78] helped teach my Uncle Severo how to weave and then how to improve his looms. Severo, in turn, taught my father and his brothers and sisters. Mier instructed Severo to keep the gears on his loom but to throw the rest of it away. One innovation, which had to do with using four treadles for a two-harness loom instead of two, spread the weight more evenly over the harnesses and thus facilitated the entire weaving process by keeping the shed open. Another Mier improvement employed wire heddles instead of string ones. The heddles, housed in the harnesses, separate the warp thread so that the shuttle or the spools of thread used as weft can pass through. Wire heddles made dressing the loom easier and faster.

"Of course, the skill of the weaver didn't have to be so great. The conscious effort on the dealer's part was always to encourage the weaver to weave faster in order to bring the price of weaving down, an aspect of industrialization that occurred at every phase of the Industrial Revolution. Using commercial yarn was another time and

Figure with Shadow, 1990, by Irvin Trujillo. Commercial 4-ply, natural-dyed weft with 2-ply warp, 54 x 75 inches. Collection of the Albuquerque Museum.

cost-saving device promoted by the blanket dealers to increase the weaver's production."

LISA TRUJILLO

Curled up in a chair, Lisa reflects on her own development as a weaver:

"I have always woven pieces that pushed the boundary of my abilities. Within a couple of months of beginning to weave, I had completed a two-piece seamed textile that was clearly an ambitious project for a beginner. I even wove a Saltillo my first year. Of course, the Trujillo men, Irvin and his father, were always there to fix my loom if something went wrong, and it helped enormously to have this support in the beginning.

"What I have woven has changed considerably over the years. Now I am currently fascinated with pattern and its variations within the piece. There are endless ways for a weaver to establish a pattern at the loom. I have spent a long time looking at the old pieces—the classic Saltillos, Rio Grandes, and Chimayós—to see how the designs were achieved. The manner in which pattern was established is especially interesting in Chimayós. The process of studying these classic designs has taught me everything regarding how designs are carried out.

"Chimayó weaving typically calls for very strong colors—black and white against a red background. I'm more conservative with color than Irvin and use color in a more feminine and perhaps harmonious way. I use colors that personally appeal to me; they become an expression of my state of mind. For pieces I call 'rainbow weavings' I often will use leftover yarns generated by other weavers, creating from these random colors weavings that are filled with energy and excitement [see *Pleiades,* page 35].

"Weaving is a very honest thing. It's hard to avoid having your own style. I alternate between weaving spontaneous pieces, such as the rainbow variations, and more carefully conceived ones. In this, I've always had a certain rhythm. I'll do a complicated piece, followed by a few easier ones, and then jump in way over my head again. One very good reason for weaving a more complicated textile is that it is intellectually more challenging. When I make the time commitment, I can become deeply involved. The design demands of such a piece create an incredible focus. (A simpler piece, by the way, isn't necessarily easier; it just doesn't take as long.) I don't see myself as forcing the complexity but rather as just allowing it to happen. What is woven is exactly what needs to be woven at that time. So if I'm weaving something complex with a lot of spools and a nice rhythm, it's extremely satisfying—both challenging and diverting. As soon as one can get beyond a 20 x 20–inch textile, there is room to really make a statement, especially with a Saltillo or Vallero. This is why I love Saltillo.

"I have woven two complex Saltillos, and spun yarn for a third while pregnant with my first child, Adam. The complete focus I formerly

Pleiades, 1988, by Lisa Trujillo. Commercial 4-ply, natural-dyed weft with 2-ply warp, 36 x 65 inches. Private collection.

could bring to the loom is nearly impossible to achieve now with two children. I like to think that this lifestyle will give them greater choices and opportunities than I imagined for myself as a child. It presents such a complicated mix of activites, and constantly confronts us with a variety of skills, ideas, and people.

"Irvin tells of Native Americans who would stare at the design in a Saltillo to invoke visions and direct peyote journeys because the designs are all so mesmerizing. I can imagine a million different possibilities when I sit down to weave a Saltillo, and get so involved in the process that the end result is magical. This kind of weaving is also very spiritual and the pace much slower. While I always try to achieve this kind of relationship with my weaving, in the complicated pieces it is more likely to occur.

"Before weaving *Hyperactive* in 1984, I had woven pieces in the thousand dollar range, but *Hyperactive* was much more complex. Irvin and his dad chided me for putting so much time into it, but I felt the time investment was very worthwhile. People were willing to pay well for a piece that contained very fine workmanship. As a result, the process that I had embarked on evolved from weaving as craft to weaving as art."

Adam's Time, *1991. Commercial 4-ply, natural-dyed weft with 2-ply warp, 36 x 63 inches.*

"THE BASIC PROCEDURE for any plain, two-harness weaving is to open the shed, throw the shuttle through (making sure there is sufficient weft thread), then change the shed and beat to pack the thread in tight. Tapestry probably originated with the earliest weavers; in two-harness weaving it exists any time there is a design other than a stripe. In the case of classic Saltillo, the early tapestry work was probably tedious—very, very fine threads, perhaps three times as many across the width of the loom as one might employ today.

"Tapestry constitutes anything with a discontinuous weft, so the weft does not move from left to right with the passage of the shuttle; instead of the shuttle I move spools, one for every color. Looking from right to left or the reverse across the warp of the textile, every time there is a change of color in tapestry the weaver has moved a spool to create it.

"To form a design in Rio Grande tapestry, three different angles are employed: *despacio,* which takes in one warp thread at a time creating an obtuse angle; *recio,* which in taking in two warp threads at a time creates a more acute angle; and, in Rio Grande weaving, the dovetail, which creates a vertical ninety-degree angle. Whatever the design outcome in Rio Grande tapestry, it is achieved one thread at a time, moving vertically up the loom in despacio, recio, or dovetail.

"In order to be a really good weaver, one must be able to see one's mistakes quickly as well as to imagine the desired end result. For this, I use a lot of math. I have to be able to see how many repeats I'm going to make before the design gets this far vertically or that far horizontally. Is the design going to touch the border? Will I have to turn it around at some point? How many times do I have to turn it around?

In other words, I can't just pretend that it looks great; I have to take responsibility for it.

"Because the designs that I create have to be exceptional, I am always willing to take chances. I have woven pieces where I've walked away and thought, 'it just doesn't have the energy I want, it's too tight,' mostly because these pieces have been too well thought out, too preconceived.

"Weaving is everything to me, complete in every way. It is the most perfect expression of myself that I can imagine in that it is logical, emotional, and meditative. This last aspect addresses rhythm and pattern and keeping the pattern going."

"IRVIN HAS ALWAYS felt that spinning was a female occupation—his grandmother, Francisquita, for example, was a great spinner—and so he was never really interested in learning much about it. I learned to spin on an Ashford wheel, which was frustrating at first, but I knew that if I had patience, I could master it. One night, after my first spinning lesson, I just sat down and began to spin.

Lisa Trujillo at the loom.

"Spinning is also magic, different from weaving in that it's far from intellectual and very relaxing. I've tried to spin all kinds of different materials, including silk, which is a most luxurious experience. I've spun cashgora (part cashmere and part Angora goat), Angora rabbit, mohair (Angora goat), alpaca, and llama. As for wool, I've spun really fine merino, Columbian, Cotswold, Rambouillet (really crimpy stuff), Lincoln, Border Leicester, California Red, and lots and lots of churro.

"Some of the finer wools are really greasy. If I have to wash this lanolin out, then I have to card or comb the fleece, and I really don't like doing either one. It is physically hard work, and if I can avoid it, I do. Churro, though, has a superb luster but is not greasy. I like its texture, which is not too crimpy. The lanolin of the churro fleece feels good and melts in my hand. The fibers grow into each other well enough that the whole fleece has a really nice continuity.

"Irvin's family talks about traveling from Chimayó to Trampas on horseback over the Borrego Mesa in the early twentieth century with a couple of sacks of chile in tow to trade with the sheepherders for fleeces for the winter's spinning. The family owned about twenty sheep at the time, a number that was still insufficient to meet their spinning needs. Today we buy our wool for handspinning from Cerro Mojino, where we are assured of getting high-quality, authentic churro, just like the churro the earliest Trujillos used."

"I THINK OF WEAVING as integration in that it never supports one highly developed skill over another," Lisa continues. "Rather, it is the process of allowing the skills of creativity, imagination, vision, mathematics, rhythm, and pattern to come through. I also think of weaving as process rather than product. The twentieth century is moving too fast; weaving is a process that allows us to slow down.

"I do not weave to project my ego but to submerge it in an artistic process channeled through me, not by me. There is a humility in this process and a wonder and magic in the result. It is nurturing and healing and provides a spiritual connection to nature and to life.

"Centinela gives us the opportunity to use the values and skills of the past—those of the generalist over the specialist, integration over specialization, process over product, and spending time rather than saving it—to create a meaningful present."

THE ESSENCE OF Centinela Traditional Arts is innovation within the evolution of traditional forms. In 1992, in response to a New York client, a board member of the American Craft Museum who wanted a 12 x 12–foot pan-Southwestern textile of a single width (see page 64), Irvin engineered drawings for a textile design that perfectly suited the client by incorporating Navajo, Hopi, Mexican, Spanish, and Rio Grande elements and even drew up plans to fabricate the oversize loom necessary to create such a piece. Centinela has produced more than thirty large textile commissions since that time.

"Some of our weavings hang from the ceiling," Irvin explains, "not only to open the eyes of our clients and give them a perspective but also to continue to educate our own weavers.

"Lisa's weaving is more formal; mine is more experimental, both mathematically and with form. Lisa has an extraordinary skill that I don't have, and I have a skill that she doesn't have. We find that we can do more as a group than we can do alone and thus, for us, Centinela is a marvelous advantage. We approach our work individually, but Centinela is a place where we can think and show together.

"My cousins left the area for college; they never learned how to weave or ever seemed interested in it. But now they are beginning to return to Chimayó and have started to show an interest in Hispanic weaving. They come over from time to time and ask if I can help them warp their loom, but perhaps they are looking for more than that. I believe that weaving can put us in touch with our past and, through this past, in touch with ourselves.

"In my own weaving, I try to examine my connection to the previous generation. This is why I have to be centered. I'm not really trying to preserve the tradition of weaving as much as to explore new areas that push the boundaries of the tradition. I don't weave to try to impress somebody with a fancy design. I weave because it soothes my soul."

ORIGINS AND DESIGN SYSTEMS OF RIO GRANDE WEAVING

Pursuing riches in the form of gold, Juan de Oñate all but ignored the true wealth that surrounded him—the very land on which he trod and the herd of churro sheep, numbering 4,000, that followed him in 1598 into Spain's "Kingdom of New Mexico." The southern portion, the Rio Abajo, where the land fell away into broad flat plains that could support enormous flocks with access to both water from the Rio Grande River and forage, perfectly exemplified this.[79]

Churro sheep thrived in the New World because the females had strong maternal instincts and carefully raised their young. By 1807 the size of the *cordones,* or sheep caravans, departing from the New Mexico provinces every August and November had swelled to 15,000, causing U.S. Army explorer Lieutenant Zebulon Montgomery Pike to attest in an internal report to the military that the annual export of sheep from New Mexico numbered approximately 30,000 head. By 1832 the livestock tally of sheep and goats had grown to a quarter of a million, making sheep "the staple production of New Mexico, and the principal article of exportation."[80]

Sheep were not the only article exported, however. Though handspun, handwoven, and hand-dyed Rio Grande textiles—sarapes and frazadas—were woven primarily for the homes in which they were made, many also were exported south to New Spain via the trade fairs at the center of Mexico's commerce. Fairs were held in several cities at different times of the year to accommodate the traders and merchants who attended them.[81] Beginning in the late seventeenth century, the great Saltillo fair was held each year in September in Saltillo, Mexico. Merchants and traders traveled from all over Mexico to procure items that were then sold at the fairs of San Bartólome, San Juan de los Lagos, and Chihuahua.[82]

In December at the Chihuahua fair, goods from New Mexico, which had its own trade fairs—pelts, robes, and basketry—were exchanged for the woven goods offered by the Spanish and the Pueblos.[83] Participants in the "Chihuahua fair banded together in a great caravan for mutual protection against the attacks of the Chichameca [Indians] through whose territory they had to pass."[84] The caravan was usually provided with a military escort for those traveling from Northern New Mexico and journeyed six hundred miles for the opportunity to trade in Chihuahua.

During the Mexican period, 1821 to 1845, *efectos del país,* a term connoting locally produced items of which handwoven textiles comprised a large percentage, were traded in Mexico. Trading efectos became "an established and lucrative" occupation by 1821.[85] For example, in 1838,

Jerga, 1988, by Irvin Trujillo. Two widths seamed, commercial worsted with natural indigo dye and undyed natural weft on a 3-ply commercial berber warp, 84 x 84 inches. Private collection.

Rio Grande, c. 1830, weaver unknown. Handspun, natural-dyed churro weft with handspun warp, 48 x 74 inches.
A Pedro Garcia family heirloom, given to Jacobo and Isabelle Trujillo on their wedding.

10,000 woven items were shipped to Mexico from New Mexico. In 1840, this figure had grown to 23,000.[86] Other than woven goods, "efectos included wool, piñon nuts, salt, buffalo hides, elk hides, antelope hides, bear hides, mountain lion hides and beaver hides."[87] In exchange for their many exported native goods, New Mexicans acquired printed cottons or calicoes, linens, woolen articles, windowpanes, tools, pins, needles, threads, and every conceivable dry good.[88] The vigorous commercial life that prevailed in New Mexico greatly influenced the weaving industry and the exchange of design ideas and dye materials through cross-fertilization.

Probably the most important utilitarian fabric woven by New Mexicans was the inexpensive and multipurpose textile called jerga, derived from the Portuguese *xerga,* or the French *serge,* meaning "serve" or "sackcloth."[89] Jerga, in the form of "handspun lengths of twill-woven plaids or checks,"[90] was a loose weave that required less wool than other textiles and was thus less time consuming to produce. It was frequently laid upon the packed earthen floors of the adobe homes prevalent in the area. Snakeweed (*yerba de la víbora*) was sometimes placed under the jerga to discourage mice and insects and, with straw, to provide a semblance of padding.[91] A pleasing complement of light and dark colors (white with black or brown) was common for early jerga produced in New Mexico. Later jerga demonstrated a fondness for red with loud background colors such as hot pink or orange.[92] The twill weave used in jerga requires four treadles and four harnesses as opposed to the two employed for the flat weave of blankets. Cheaper dyes and coarser fibers often were reserved for this woven floor covering.[93]

"The most commonly produced, widely distributed and simply designed of the nineteenth-century New Mexican Spanish goods," suggests textile historian Dorothy Boyd Bowen, was the Rio Grande blanket.[94] This blanket, or frazada, was unique to the New Mexican culture, and no "documented examples" from California, Arizona, Texas, or northern Mexico approximate the Rio Grande.[95] "It was woven in the settlements and ranches along the Rio Grande and its tributaries for three centuries, and was a staple of the economy as well as a necessity for survival. . . . It was traded far south into Mexico, east in the United States, west to California, and in all directions to the Indians."[96] These blankets were worn during the day wrapped around the shoulders and used for bedding at night. Until about 1860, it was the custom for wealthy men to wear the blankets while the poor wore jackets of jerga.[97]

Rio Grande "textiles were woven on the narrow (two-harness) treadle loom either in two widths . . . or in one width with multiple center warps, in weft-faced plain weave or tapestry weave."[98] It was difficult to match exactly the two lengths of blanket, and so the double-woven technique was developed, which used two sets of warps, kept separate by the regulation of the tie-up of four harnesses.[99] The blanket was woven folded, two harnesses devoted to each layer. Unfolded, it had recognizable paired warps that created a slight ridge down the center.

Classic Saltillo sarape, late 18th century, weaver unknown. Handspun, natural-dyed weft on cotton(?) warp, 50 x 90 inches. Private collection.

Natural dyes, particularly indigo blue, "were used for a majority of early Spanish blankets," and the presence of indigo usually indicated a blanket of high quality.[100] "The design system of the early indigo-dyed blankets is based on a five- or seven-band layout. Each band section is composed of smaller stripes in varying widths, with the band repeated two or three times in the blanket."[101] Typically, a white stripe began the blanket and became the field for the other stripes woven in indigo and brown.[102]

Shortly after Spain began to colonize New Mexico, workshops for "the commercial treadle loom production of woolen goods were established."[103] In the early years, Santa Fe was a leading center for production and export of woven cloth. By 1790, however, weaving in the vicinity of Rio Arriba, which included Santa Fe, had declined severely at the same time that it began to flourish in Rio Abajo with as many as one-third of heads of household declaring themselves involved in the production of textiles.[104]

In fact, the decline of textile production in the north was so severe that government officials decided to contract with two expert weavers and guild members from Mexico, Don Ygnacio Ricardo Bazán and his brother, Don Juan, who traveled to Santa Fe, where they worked for the next two years to upgrade the weaving skills among the younger population.[105]

The Bazán brothers also are credited with introducing a simplified format of the Saltillo sarape, another design system of Rio Grande textiles. The Rio Grande Saltillo was inspired by the classic Mexican Saltillo sarape often considered one of the most finely woven textiles in the world and thought to have originated with the Tlaxcalan Indians who lived near present-day Puebla, Mexico.[106]

Bitter enemies of the Aztec people, when the Spanish first arrived in the Gulf of Mexico, the Tlaxcalans sided with them against the Aztecs and helped to overwhelm them. As a result, in later years they were given special status by the Spanish. In 1591, they were asked to colonize the town of Saltillo and by their presence to tame the nearby Chichameca Indians. In Saltillo, they were allocated a special barrio by the Spanish, San Esteban de Nuevo Tlaxcala, from which the Saltillo sarape originated. It was native, not Spanish, though woven on Spanish looms from churro wool.[107]

The result of these labors, the classic Mexican Saltillo, was a finely woven, labor intensive, very elaborate fabric that took an estimated one to two years to weave and thus became a valuable status symbol in Mexico worn by the *ricos,* the symbol of a gentleman, and later emblematic of Mexican nationalism. The formal design system of the Saltillo sarape consisted of a border running along all four sides of a rectangle with a vertically oriented background and a central serrated diamond or occasional lozenge shape.[108]

New Mexican weavers tried to emulate their counterparts from Saltillo, and by 1830,[109] at the same time that selective design components were becoming incorporated into Rio Grande striped blankets,

Vallero, c. 1930, 20 x 27 inches, weaver unknown. Commercial 4-ply weft with commercial dyes and 2-ply wool warp. This one-star Vallero is the kind Teresita Trujillo Jaramillo was known to have woven.

Vallero, c. 1890, 24 x 30 inches, weaver unknown. Commercial 3-ply weft with commercial dyes and cotton warp. Isidoro Trujillo traded sacks of green chile to sheepherders in Panchuela, part of the Sangre de Cristo Mountains east of Chimayó, for pieces such as this.

a simplified Saltillo sarape also began to appear.

Some Rio Grande Saltillos employ only the background design of the Saltillo sarape to create an overall pattern. Others feature only a central diamond motif that radiates out from the center of the textile to the top and bottom. The Rio Grande Saltillo is also more coarsely woven than the Saltillo sarape.

Other developments occurred during the nineteenth century that helped to evolve the sheep and textile industry in New Mexico. Anglo sheep ranchers, especially in the Rio Abajo, decided that the churro sheep produced both insufficient wool and meat and attempted to "upgrade" the breed by introducing the French strains of merino and Rambouillet. In actuality, this hurt the caliber of handspun wool in New Mexico because the Rambouillet wool was kinky and unsuitable for hand spinning, and the wool of both French strains was much greasier and thus harder to clean.

During the 1850s and 1860s, the introduction of the sawmill and the arrival of milled lumber in New Mexico contributed to looms with smaller frames. Metal reeds imported over the Santa Fe Trail replaced wooden ones, affecting the width of the woven piece and the method of production.[110] By the 1870s, commercial dyes were introduced and imported commercial yarns such as the aniline-dyed yarns from Germantown, Pennsylvania, became available. Many of these new materials became more accessible because of the railroad, which arrived in New Mexico in 1880.[111]

The new yarn products first impacted the Rio Grande tradition in a blanket called the Vallero or Trampas-Vallero, named after the towns Las Trampas and El Valle, which are situated to the north of Chimayó. Trampas-Vallero blankets are characterized by distinctive eight-pointed stars—one in each corner of the blanket and one in the center. The Trampas-Vallero blanket first appeared around 1865 at a time when fur trappers were trading in this area. Valleros also were traded with the Plains Indians.[112]

Historians question the origins of the Vallero blanket and its eight-pointed Vallero star. Some people think it originated in Mexico or South America, but the form of the Trampas-Vallero weavings is somewhat different from the Mexican-derived Saltillo. There is also a possible connection to the star used in Moorish architecture. The American quilt employs an eight-pointed star called the LeMoyne Star, suggesting the possibility of American quilts being traded into the Trampas–El Valle area. Valleros are as colorful as the Navajo Germantown weavings because they evolved during the Germantown period. These textiles feature colors such as kelly green, red-orange, yellows, golds, and purples pitched to a high intensity.

The Trujillos believe that the Vallero blanket made its way to Chimayó from the Montoya family in Truchas and El Valle. It was introduced into Chimayó through a Martina Montoya living in Truchas who worked for Severo Jaramillo and who taught Teresita Trujillo Jaramillo how to weave it.

Trampas-Vallero, 1984, by Jacobo O. Trujillo. Handspun, natural-dyed weft with 2-ply warp, 54 x 84 inches. Yarn spun by Jacobo's wife, Isabelle, and dyed by his son, Irvin. Private collection.

In the 1880s, a further innovation, cotton "string" warp, which replaced handspun wool warp, was adopted by both Hispano and Navajo weavers. Cotton warp appeared in the first Chimayó blankets, which are a composite of both the Rio Grande stripe and the Saltillo diamond and comprise the final design system of Rio Grande weaving.

A Chimayó weaver at his loom, from a vintage postcard.

The evolution of the Chimayó blanket was tied to the New Mexican tourist trade. The tourist trade was fueled by ideas inherent in the Arts and Crafts Movement, which began in England at the mid-nineteenth century and, crossing the Atlantic, arrived in the Southwest sometime around 1875. Tourists to the Southwest perceived the indigenous arts and crafts of the American Indian as the embodiment of Arts and Crafts ethos and first sought Navajo weavings to decorate their Victorian houses. "The Chimayó-style weaving, cheaper to make and woven with commercially prepared materials, "evolved to fill a gap or gaps" in the Navajo textile market.[113]

To market the Chimayó weavings, a curious strategy developed that implied that the name "Chimayó" was that of "yet another tribe of weaving Indians."[114] Because the Chimayó blankets could be bought for one-third the cost of a Navajo weaving of the same size, this strategy hoped to appeal to the buyer who could not afford the more expensive Navajo weaving. At other times, when convenient for marketing needs, "the Mexican-ness" of Chimayó weaving was stressed. These strategies so blurred the real identity of the Chimayó blanket that an article published in the Smithsonian Institution's *American Museum of Natural History Journal* in 1912 read: "Chimayó blankets made by Chimayó Indians of northern New Mexico, who are now practically extinct, are thought to be the connecting link between Navajo and Saltillo (i.e. Mexican) weaving."[115] The Chimayó blanket also began to appeal to those customers interested in a more supple textile for draping, unlike the Navajo weavings, which took on the affinities of a heavy and closely woven floor rug.[116]

The early Chimayó-style textile was smaller than the traditional Rio Grande frazada of the nineteenth century. For example, rectangular textiles were sometimes woven for pillow tops or portieres. Saltillo design elements, distilled and simplified, often were employed. The early Chimayó textiles also sometimes lacked a central motif, contained an asymmetrical layout, and imparted a fractioned, unbalanced feeling[117]:

> Partial motifs entering the design field from the side or appearing at its corners were not unusual. The smallest of pieces dispensed with the striped transverse bands at top and bottom and larger pieces summarized these bands into a simpler pattern of broad stripes.[118]

Motifs designed to invoke a sense of the Native American such as bows, arrows, and the swastika, "touted as the Native American good luck symbol,"[119] also were used.

Over the years, the Chimayó blanket evolved into what textile historian Suzanne Baizerman suggests is the prototypical Chimayó weaving:

> . . . a rectangular textile featuring transverse bands at top and bottom and a large central motif. The bands are elaborately striped with ticking and follow a stan-

Jake's Gift, c. 1975, by Jacobo O. Trujillo. Commercial 4-ply weft with 2-ply warp, 54 x 87 inches. Private collection.

Woven as a teaching device and gift for Irvin, Jake included all elements of Chimayó weaving. There are designs within the stripes, corner elements, jaspes, *and primary and secondary designs. There are step designs,* despacio, recio, *and curves. Stripes have solids, alternating rounds, and paladares. These sinuous turns influenced Lisa's later work.*

dard though complex formula. The central motif is usually an elaborated diamond. Sometimes an elaborated hourglass shape is used instead. The elaborations occur at the top and sides of the central motif and are what weaver Irvin Trujillo terms the "base" and the "wings." Frequently outlining is used. A pictorial representation, such as a bird, might assume the position of a central motif.

> As the size of the rectangle increases, so does the number of auxiliary motifs, placed on either side of the central motif. First are added motifs that are variations on the central motif, reduced in size. Then additional space-filling motifs, such as *jaspes*, the faint parallel, horizontal lines which form patterns unrelated to the central and auxiliary motifs, would be added. The space is filled in a balanced way and the motifs arranged rhythmically.[120]

By the 1930s the limited palette of the early Chimayó blankets (red, black, gray, and white to emulate popular Native American colors) had evolved into a broader and more intense palette that included bright red, orange, turquoise, and bright blue in addition to gray, white, and black.[121]

Anglo patrons such as Mary Austin and Frank Applegate, who started the Spanish Colonial Arts Society in 1925, came to "dismiss [the Chimayó] as an inferior tourist item"[122] and to endorse instead the Rio Grande blanket as an example of traditional Hispanic weaving. Yet the Chimayó blanket has endured and evolved to the present day with its own particular design integrity, which only recently has been threatened by the influx of "Chimayó-style" blankets woven in and imported from Mexico by the El Paso Saddle Blanket Company and by others who are trying to undersell authentic Rio Grande textiles.

In an effort to safeguard and preserve the integrity and authenticity of Rio Grande weavings, Centinela Traditional Arts asks weavers to sign their pieces. There is also a shop imprimatur whereby a Centinela weaving is both begun and finished with warp. Limited editions from Centinela, in numbers of five only, are impressed with a small silver tag bearing the insignia "Centinela Traditional Arts, Chimayó, New Mexico."

The photos that follow illustrate some of Irvin and Lisa Trujillo's strongest, most important pieces. They are personal favorites for various reasons, and a brief commentary describes each weaving's significance from the artist's perspective. This group of fourteen textiles represents selected highlights from work produced throughout their weaving careers.

Hyperactive, 1984, by Lisa Trujillo. Commercial 4-ply, natural-dyed weft with 2-ply warp , 36 x 60 inches. Collection of Robert B. Riley.

This piece was woven in response to Irvin's innovative description of his idea of ikat in the context of tapestry. I loved his idea. I think it says a lot about us that what I wove from his description of his plans is so very different than what he executed in Littoral Equinox *[see page 57]. My piece uses small ikat-dyed diamonds in the background with piquietes throughout.*

Tellin' Tales, 1998, by Lisa Trujillo. Handspun, natural-dyed weft with 2-ply warp, 54 x 84 inches.

This comes from my great joy resuming weaving after a long, stressful administrative period. I felt the piece reflected ancient mythologies of which I was only vaguely aware, and others responded to its exotic foreign look. At the time, people were telling me of the deep, subtle symbols of Navajo weavers. Its name is true of all of our weavings.

Devotion, 1987, by Lisa Trujillo. Two widths seamed, handspun churro weft (52 threads per inch) on linen warp (12 ends per inch), 58 x 88 inches.

I wanted to weave a Saltillo ever since seeing the show at the Wheelwright Museum on our honeymoon. A fine Saltillo demands a very fine yarn, which I was able to spin after a year or two. For the warp, I chose linen. We set up a narrow loom with a size-12 reed. I dyed the weft yarns with cochineal and indigo, our most lightfast dyes. When midway through the first half, I had to decide what belonged in the center; the heart represented the faith that I was doing the right thing. A weaving this detailed takes so much time and focus. I had to prove to myself, and to my husband and his father, that weaving a complex piece was worthwhile.

Passion in the Web, 1989, by Lisa Trujillo. Two widths seamed, handspun, natural-dyed churro weft (52 threads per inch) with 2-ply warp (12 ends per inch), 58 x 82 inches. Collection of Fran and Carol Mullin.

The ideas I wove into Passion in the Web *are a lot about continuity and connectedness, about the value of simplicity and complexity and that they can both coexist comfortably. I took pleasure in the natural variations in the handspun and occasionally chose to emphasize it rather than hide it.*

I used cool "intellectual" blue for the border to hold back the passion of the red. White acts as the connecting color for all of it—for purity and spirit and honesty. The last big concept was the "invisible" center that ties it all together, not really visible and yet felt through tension between the elements pointing toward the center.

You Can Never Go Home Again, 1988, by Lisa Trujillo. Commercial 4-ply, natural-dyed weft with 2-ply warp, 36 x 72 inches. Private collection.

Irvin and I had just returned from six months in Santa Fe where we decided to rearrange our priorities and forge a distinct, new identity free from the constraints of the family system by building a new studio. I wove this piece in response to a home environment that had changed on both literal and figurative levels. Weaving in a new studio, our own, made all the difference in the world. You Can Never Go Home Again, *a rainbow piece using remnant yarns, was filled with many subtle colors that revealed themselves to me in the natural light from the newly installed skylight.*

Bubbles, 1993, by Lisa Trujillo. Handspun, natural indigo-dyed, and natural undyed weft with 2-ply warp, 50 x 72 inches.

This was woven during and after my pregnancy with daughter Emily, born May 21, 1993. I couldn't exert as much tension on the warp during pregnancy as afterward, which presented a big problem in later matching the two sections of this textile. Conforming the two shifted ikat-dyed yarns in the background to the tapestry border was even more challenging—perhaps the most difficult technical problem I've dealt with so far in weaving.

Todas Madres, 1996, by Lisa Trujillo. Handspun, natural-dyed, and undyed weft with commercial 2-ply warp, 72 x 96 inches.

This subtly colored piece addresses motherhood and femininity and the links in a generational chain of events. Todas Madres *refers back to our parents and also forward toward the future. Femininity is not a structural, linear thing but rather about bending and adapting, just as fibers that twist together and then move apart epitomize the female construct. Women are usually the fiber artists in American culture, but in Hispanic culture men play an equal role.*

Littoral Equinox, 1985, by Irvin Trujillo. Commercial 4-ply, natural-dyed weft with 2-ply warp, 54 x 82 inches. Private collection.

I had a dream in Dodge City, Kansas, where I was conducting some economic surveys. The dream was a truly inspired design for ikat tapestry; the resist process of ikat itself, which the design necessitated, took a year to learn. This piece uses figure, random, and shifted ikat combined with tapestry to represent elements of earth, fire, air, and water. "Littoral" means seaside, and an equinox marks a transit of the heavens in which the day and night are of equal length, signaling the progression from one season to the next. At the time, I was changing my career from engineer to full-time weaver, which was very significant for me.

Spider from Mars, 1988, by Irvin Trujillo. Commercial 4-ply, natural-dyed weft with 2-ply warp, 54 x 76 inches. Collection of the Museum of American History, Smithsonian Institution.

Inspired by a Brazilian headdress and a David Bowie album, Ziggy Stardust and the Spiders from Mars, *this piece depicts a story about the weaving industry. In it, the weavers are represented by birds and the scholars by fish. The fish are always bickering with each other and speculating as to the history of weaving, just as I speculate on Valleros and Saltillos and their evolution.*

Faceto, 1989, by Irvin Trujillo. Commercial 4-ply, natural-dyed weft with 2-ply warp, 54 x 30 inches. Collection of Marjorie Weinberg-Berman.

An abstract of black-and-white interlocking forms, faceto *is a double entendre. There are many facets within the textile ("faceto" in Spanish means "conceit") and this references the duality or ambiguity in viewing the light/dark patterning, in hanging the piece upside down or even diagonally, and, of course, in the identical image front and back.*

Additionally, Faceto *is a study, woven to explore numerical coordinates using rise and run to get from one point to the other.*

Rio Grande Fusion, 1989, by Irvin Trujillo. Commercial 4-ply, natural-dyed weft with 2-ply warp, 54 x 84 inches. Private collection.

This study of the Fibonacci number series within vertical and horizontal tapestry work illustrates color blending regulated by numerical sequences. The corners contain Spanish elements typically found in a classic 1860s Rio Grande blanket. The design at either end of the Saltillo diamond and the chain of flowers in the center reflect a more Chimayó-style influence.

Named after what became a bogus cold fusion discovery at the University of Utah, its colors—from cochineal, indigo, chamisa, and madder root—fuse to form a Rio Grande blanket from disparate elements. It was chosen for the Spanish Market poster in 1992.

La Entriega, 1991, by Irvin Trujillo. Commercial 4-ply, natural-dyed weft with 2-ply warp, 54 x 82 inches. Private collection.

This is the piece I worked on the winter after my father died. It was a study of numerical color sequences that go in and out of phase with each other in the border. La Entriega *has several connotations, including introduction of the bride to the community and the sponsors' delivering of a baptized child or newly wedded couple to their respective parents. In a Hispanic village such as Chimayó, it also refers to the delivery of the village patron saint to its sponsors for the new year.*

In this case, I offered this textile to the community of Spanish Market in 1991. I was surprised to win the Judges Grand Award.

Una Pieza Galactica, 1991, by Irvin Trujillo. Commercial 4-ply, natural-dyed weft with 2-ply warp, 54 x 56 inches. Collection of Jack and Jessica Powell.

This refers to the limits that I have placed on myself in the past, limits created by my misperceptions of how I fit into the world. By learning to let limitations give way to new goals and new aspirations, we create a new context in which to define the "self." This is a fluid rather than a rigid process.

My mother used to always tell me "the sky is the limit." But to me, the sky was simply the blue I saw every day above me.

Una Pieza Galactica *can be hung with the blue on top or on the bottom, wherever the viewer might like his personal sky. This piece was part of the* Chispas *exhibit at the Heard Museum, Phoenix, from 1991 to 1993.*

La Vereda, 1995, by Irvin Trujillo. Commercial 4-ply weft with 2-ply warp, commercial red, teal blue, and kelly green yarns are commercial-dyed, all others natural-dyed, 54 x 84 inches.

La Vereda *is an assemblage of vehicles that depict the stages of a man's life: the sports car, the gaiety of young manhood; the truck, pragmatic middle age; at the end of life, a hearse carries the body to the grave site. The space shuttle represents the transport of the soul, and the dove indicates the afterlife. Finally there is a Tree of Life in which one "old bird" talks to another about the journey.*

The design field introduces triangles at either end of the blanket that are combined with the simple stripes of the chief's blanket. The brilliant colors of this piece typify the Vallero style: red, teal blue, kelly green, chamisa (yellow), peach leaves (tan), madder root (orange), and brazilwood (rust).

CENTINELA TRADITIONAL ARTS

by Lisa Trujillo

IRVIN TRUJILLO IS A seventh-generation weaver and Lisa a first, which suggests something of the broad diversity among the weavers at Centinela Traditional Arts. Centinela weavers are professionals. Most of them weave full-time in their own homes and specialize in the designs and widths they prefer to weave. While we usually contract with individuals, we often end up working with entire families of weavers—at the present time, the Trujillo and Vigil families (distant cousins), two Valdez families, and a family of Romeros. Almost everyone who weaves or sews for Centinela has someone related to them also working for us. We are proud to continue the tradition of a local extended family of weavers.

Rudy Valdez is a third-generation weaver who lives in Española and weaves with his whole family. He learned to weave from his sister after incurring a serious back injury and in turn taught his wife Ginnie to weave. He particularly enjoys designing textiles. Ginnie and the Valdez daughters, Valorie Valdez and Victoria Verry, weave 20- and 30-inch widths. Rudy's son, Rudy Lee Valdez, and his brother Joseph help in weaving our large-scale custom rugs, as well as blanket-weight coats. Experienced in a variety of styles and widths, the Valdezes are primarily weavers of the Chimayó style.

Dimas and Dulcinea Vigil come from a long tradition of weavers in Cundiyó and Rio Chiquito who are related to the Trujillos. Dimas has been weaving for fifty-three years and remembers the early days when his parents raised sheep and sheared, spun, and dyed wool. His wife Dulcinea has been weaving for forty-eight years. Originally from Rio Chiquito, she too remembers seasons of tending sheep, shearing, spinning, and dyeing in addition to weaving blankets for home use.

Dimas is a master of design in the Chimayó style; we use his designs in the Chimayó coats. Dimas and Dulcinea, along with their daughter Lourdes, who has spent twenty-one years at the loom, weave 15-, 30-, 36-, and 48-inch widths. For several years, Lourdes's mentor was Irvin's father, Jake, from whom she learned many weaving techniques.

Gloria Montoya weaves complex 20-inch widths, including a "Tree of Life" and a "Zigzag Modern" pattern of her own invention. She also weaves 30-inch widths as well as Vallero and Saltillo blankets.

Dorothy and Cecilia Gallegos are a mother-and-daughter team; they weave 10- and 15-inch textiles. Rebecca Duran is a 20-inch width weaver with a distinctive personal style that combines delicate design elements and deep colors. Jerry Trujillo, another relative, weaves on a variety of looms in both blanket and rug weights. His brother Albino specializes in vests for Centinela. Pita Trujillo, their sister and the shop manager, helps to coordinate all the weavers, as well as the weavings

Facing page: Pan-Southwestern commission (detail), 1993, by Irvin Trujillo. Handspun, hand-dyed churro wool weft with 2-ply warp, 12 x 12 feet. Private collection.

and elements of fabrication. Our sewing contractors, Angie Garcia, Barbara Quintana, Dianne Vigil, and Agnes Lopez, along with a handful of others with specialized skills and heavy equipment, fashion from the handwoven wool fabrics the garments, pillows, and purses.

Danni Webb, one of Lisa's original apprentices in Albuquerque, is the only weaver creating nonwool clothing. Made of rayon chenille, her quechquemitl shawls illustrate her interest in the luxurious use of color and texture in clothing.

Centinela additionally displays pieces consigned by Robin Reider, Denise Miller, Margaret Herman, Martie Moreno, Carla Gomez, Chela Lightchild, Beatrice Maestas, and Rita Padilla Haufman.

A primary goal of Centinela Traditional Arts has always been to make weaving a respected and economically viable occupation. Our weaving contracts follow the standards of the Chimayó weaving industry. We strive to pay the artisans a fair price for their fine craftsmanship and try to help them reach their goals within the profession. The weavers are encouraged to sign their textiles, to acknowledge their creation and instill a level of pride in the quality of each and every weaving.

In pricing our weavings, there is the task of balancing the individual weaver's labor with a market valuation of each piece. This is relatively easy when offering certain standardized sizes and designs. It becomes a more subjective process to price the complex pieces that have taken weeks or months to complete. In the end, it's the overall aesthetic effect of the final product that matters, how the design, color, composition, and proportions all work together, as with any work of art.

Centinela Traditional Arts offers an exclusive series of editions, both limited and open, featured on pages 67-79. Some of these are classic and timeless while others are contemporary. The number of weavings in each limited edition is five. Measurements and colors will vary slightly from piece to piece within each edition due to both the unique confluence of warping and weaving and the idiosyncratic nature of the dyeing process and fleeces. Because of the importance Centinela places on originality and attribution, each textile is marked with an attached small silver tag indicating the edition number and name. Please to refer to current Centinela Traditional Arts price list for edition pricing.

1 Rio Grande Saltillo, 1995, 20 x 37 inches. *Inspired by a servant blanket from the 1860s.*

2 *Tree of Life,* 1995, 20 x 40 inches.

3 Rio Grande Saltillo, 1995, 20 x 36 inches.

These 20 x 40–inch textiles created by Gloria Montoya are commercial 4-ply, natural-dyed weft with a 2-ply warp.

4 Trampas-Vallero, 1995, 20 x 39 inches.

5 *Zigzag,* 1995, 20 x 40 inches.

6 *Ordinary Changes 1,* 1995, by Lisa Trujillo. Commercial 4-ply, natural-dyed weft with 2-ply warp, 36 x 62 inches.

7 Prototypical Chimayó, from an original design c. 1905, weaver unknown. Commercial 4-ply weft with 4-ply cotton warp, 36 x 74 inches.

8 Chimayó, 1995, by Rudy Lee Valdez. Commercial 4-ply weft with 2-ply warp, 36 x 60 inches.

9 Saltillo/Moki, 1995, by Rudy Lee Valdez. Commercial 4-ply weft with 2-ply warp, 36 x 52 inches.

10 Chimayó, 1995, by Dimas Vigil. Commercial 4-ply weft with 2-ply warp, 48 x 72 inches.

11 Moki, 1995, by Dimas Vigil. Commercial 4-ply weft with 2-ply warp, 48 x 72 inches.

12 Chimayó, 1995, by Dimas Vigil. Commercial 4-ply weft with 2-ply warp, 48 x 72 inches.

13 Rio Grande, 1995, by Dimas Vigil. Commercial 4-ply weft with 2-ply warp, 48 x 72 inches.

OE-1 Wedding blanket, from an original early 1930s design by Mercedes Trujillo. Handspun, natural-undyed weft with 2-ply warp, 48 x 72 inches. *Given to Lisa and Irvin on their marriage. Three stripes on each end indicate two parents and one child from each respective family. Center bands indicate two children to be married and the new family formed by the marriage.*

OE-2 Frazada Taos trade blanket, 1995, by Irvin Trujillo. Handspun churro, indigo-dyed and natural-undyed weft with 2-ply warp, 48 x 80 inches. *This design typifies blankets traded with Taos Indians and also pieces traded to Chihuahua and Mexico City trade fairs from the Rio Arriba.*

The four Open Edition (OE) patterns on these two pages are available in rug weight only (4 epi [ends per inch]) with handspun weft, sizes 48 x 72 and 54 x 84 inches.

OE-3 Frazada del Campo, from an original design, 1930, by Jacobo O. Trujillo. Handspun, dyed and natural weft with 2-ply warp, 54 x 86 inches.

OE-4 *La Cintura* Taos trade blanket, 1993, by Irvin Trujillo. Handspun, natural-undyed and indigo-dyed weft with 2-ply warp, 54 x 80 inches.

14 *Las Palomas,* 1986, by Jacobo O. Trujillo. Commercial 4-ply weft with 2-ply warp, 54 x 90 inches.
Inspired by a very worn piece given to Jake that featured the "whirling log" design.
Available in rug or blanket weight.

15 *Two Lines Too,* 1995, by Irvin Trujillo. Rug-weight yarns, hand-dyed with synthetic dyes, and 2-ply warp, 54 x 84 inches. *This piece shows the influence of the Navajo Third Phase chief's blanket in the corner designs and the typical scattered element background found in WPA revival pieces in the 1930s.*

16 SCAS Vallero, 1992, by Irvin Trujillo. Rug-weight yarns, hand-dyed with synthetic dyes, and 2-ply warp, 54 x 84 inches. *Original piece purchased by the Spanish Colonial Arts Society. Available in rug or blanket weight..*

LIMITED EDITIONS

17 *Old Flame,* 1995, by Irvin Trujillo. Handspun yarns with hand-dyed synthetic dyes, 54 x 84 inches.

18 Chimayó, 1945, by Jacobo O. Trujillo. Commercial 4-ply weft with commercial warp yarns, 54 x 100 inches. *Woven by Jake as a wedding present for his wife Isabelle soon after they returned from San Francisco at the end of World War II.*

19 *Lisa's Chimayó Chief's Blanket,* 1986, by Lisa Trujillo. Commercial 4-ply weft with 2-ply warp, 54 x 87 inches.
This piece is a more complex variation of a piece woven by Jake a year earlier to show Irvin and Lisa the style he had woven for Severo Jaramillo that he called "Chimayó chief's blanket."

A significant part of Centinela's work is the production of custom textiles. Thanks to Irvin Trujillo's engineering skills the shop is capable of weaving rugs up to twelve feet wide. Each textile commission request is estimated based on square footage of design, design density, and the different techniques and materials involved. Frequently yarn is dyed to provide an exact color match. A simple, elegant and long-lasting floor covering, the jerga produced at Centinela Traditional Arts and featured on the facing page is a very sturdy and hard-wearing berber wool and is priced by the square yard. Upholstery materials are woven at Centinela as well. These have been produced for furniture makers, various institutions, businesses, and individuals.

NOTES

1. Don Usner, *Sabino's Map* (Santa Fe: Museum of New Mexico Press, 1995), 57. Chimayó, according to Usner, was established in about 1776.
2. Ibid., 14.
3. Ibid., 33.
4. Ibid., 11–12.
5. Ibid.
6. A Trujillo family listed itself as original settlers at San Gabriel, the first capital of New Mexico, established September 8, 1598, by Don Juan de Oñate (*Herencia del Norte* 8, [Winter 1995]).
7. Fray Angelico Chavez, *Origins of New Mexico Families: A Geneology of the Spanish Colonial Period* (Santa Fe: Museum of New Mexico Press, 1975), xi.
8. Ibid., 107.
9. Fray Angelico Chavez suggests that a Juan de Trujillo and his wife, both natives of the Rio Abajo, returned to New Mexico with the Reconquest. Chavez also suggests that Juan de Trujillo was probably the son of old Francisco Trujillo, the only son of Diego de Trujillo. At the turn of the century, Juan moved from the Albuquerque area to Pojoaque. Chavez, 108, 296.
10. Ward Alan Minge, "Efectos del Pais: A History of Weaving Along the Rio Grande," in *Rio Grande Textiles: A New Edition of Spanish Textile Traditions of New Mexico and Colorado* (Nora Fisher, ed.) (Santa Fe: Museum of New Mexico Press, 1994), 9. Minge suggests that by 1790, as a result of Spanish Colonials developing the Rio Abajo into large sheep ranches, one-third of the heads of family there declared themselves as weavers or related to the weaving industry (that is, spin ners or carders). By contrast, in the Rio Arriba at this time, only two heads of household recorded themselves as weavers from Santa Fe and no one from the Santa Cruz area to which Chimayó, a precinct, was attached.
11. In a personal interview (spring 1996) John R. Trujillo discussed early land deeds he had encountered that indicated that Diego Trujillo was living on the road to La Azotea, better fortified even than Chimayó because the villagers could defend themselves from the top of this mesa.
12. Personal interview with John R. Trujillo, the son of Encarnación Trujillo, spring 1996.
13. Suzanne Baizerman, "Textiles, Traditions and Tourist Art: Hispanic Weaving in Northern New Mexico" (unpublished Ph.D. dissertation, Department of Anthropology, University of Minnesota, 1987), 37.
14. Marianne Stoller, "Spanish Americans, Their Servants and Sheep: A Cultural History of Weaving in Southern Colorado," in Fisher, ed., *Rio Grande Textiles,* 30–32.
15. Baizerman, 36–37.
16. *New Mexico Roots,* Marriage Records, Roll #30, AA8F, p. 1947.
17. Concepción had three brothers—Juan Felipe, Anastacio and Martín.
18. This 1848 prenuptial agreement to marry his first cousin, María Juana Antonia Ortega (age 12), can be found in *New Mexico Roots,* Marriage Records, Roll #30, AA8F, p. 1981, Frame #312.
19. Jerga was used as gunnysack material for bagging chile and corn as well as a floor covering for anterooms and *salas* or living rooms.
20. Personal interview with Mercedes Trujillo, September 3, 1995.
21. Baizerman, 50.
22. Usner, 77–78.
23. Personal interview with Mercedes Trujillo, September 3, 1995.
24. Reyes, Encarnación, Cecilio, Juan, Vidal, Manuel, Isidoro and two daughters, Nepomucena and Higinia, were born to Concepción and his wife.
25. Personal interview with Mercedes Trujillo by Irvin Trujillo, fall 1995.
26. Personal interview with Rosinaldo Trujillo, winter, 1995.
27. Jack Loeffler interview with Jacobo Trujillo, August 19, 1988.
28. Baizerman, 58.
29. Ibid., 64.
30. Ralph Emerson Twitchell, *Old Santa Fe: The Story of New Mexico's Ancient Capital* (Santa Fe: New Mexico Publishing, 1925), 408–409.
31. Baizerman, 66.
32. Ibid., 58.
33. Twitchell, 408–409.
34. Baizerman, 71.
35. Personal interview with Jonathan Batkin, director of the Wheelwright Museum, April 2, 1996.
36. Baizerman, 71.
37. Ibid., 72.
38. Baizerman (page 68) cites Ruth Laughlin Barker as a source for this information. Barker wrote an article entitled "The Craft of Chimayó," which appeared in *El Palacio* 28:6 (Santa Fe: Museum of New Mexico Press, 1930), 171.
39. Gene Doyle, "Candelario's Fabulous Curios," *The Denver Posse Westerners Monthly Roundup* 24:9 (1968): 9.
40. Baizerman, 83.
41. Sito Candelario, a form letter, December 1, 1914; Candelario Collection, History Library, Museum of New Mexico, Box 99, 1914.
42. Baizerman, 83.
43. Ibid.
44. Personal interview with Mercedes Trujillo, September 1996.
45. Ibid.
46. Personal interview with Rosinaldo Trujillo, winter 1996.
47. Personal correspondence between Tim Cordova and Lisa and Irvin Trujillo, June 3, 1996.
48. Ibid.
49. Ibid.
50. Personal interview with Rosinaldo Trujillo, winter 1996.
51. Ibid.
52. Baizerman, 94.
53. Marta Weigle, ed., *Hispanic Villages of New Mexico* (a reprint of Volume 2 of the 1935 Tewa Basin Study with supplementary materials) (Santa Fe: Lightning

Tree Press, 1974), 71.
54. Baizerman, 109.
55. Dated December 6, 1929, this price-fixing agreement may be found in the History Library, Museum of New Mexico, Santa Fe, New Mexico. A copy of this agreement is in the personal files of the Trujillo family.
56. Personal interview with Ursulo Ortiz, October 18, 1995.
57. Personal interview with Mercedes Trujillo by Irvin Trujillo, September 1995.
58. Personal interview with Irvin Trujillo, fall 1995.
59. Personal interview with Rosinaldo Trujillo, winter 1996.
60. Mary Austin, *Earth Horizon* (Boston: Houghton Mifflin Co., 1932), 358.
61. Baizerman, 61.
62. Personal ledgers of Jake Trujillo (1932–39), courtesy of the Trujillo estate and Irvin Trujillo.
63. Ibid.
64. Interview with Jake Trujillo by Jack Loeffler, August 19, 1988.
65. Jake Trujillo's ledger books, courtesy of the Trujillo estate and Irvin Trujillo.
66. Ibid.
67. Ibid.
68. Ibid.
69. Ibid.
70. Suzanne Forrest, *The Preservation of the Village: New Mexico's Hispanics and the New Deal* (Albuquerque: University of New Mexico, New Mexico Land Grant Series, 1989), 171–172.
71. Fern Lyon and Jacob Evans, *Los Alamos, the First Forty Years* (Los Alamos, NM: Los Alamos Historical Society, 1984), 49–50.
72. Ibid.
73. Phyllis K. Fisher, *Los Alamos Experience* (Tokyo and New York: Japan Publications, 1985), 253.
74. Lyon and Evans, 96.
75. Ibid., 112.
76. Mordanting is the process of attaching a salt molecule to the protein of the fiber, which then bonds with the dyestuff to create a permanent dye.
77. Discovered in 1202 by Leonardo Fibonacci, this sequence (1, 2, 3, 5, 8, 13, 21, 34, etc.) corresponds, after the fourteenth number in the series, to the ratio of the "Golden Mean," or 1:1.618. Use of this numerical sequence results in pleasing, natural proportions. Else Regensteiner, *Geometric Design in Weaving* (West Chester, PA: Schiffer Publishing, Ltd., 1986), 49.
78. From Suzanne Baizerman's correspondence to Irvin and Lisa Trujillo, 1985, corroborated by Antonio Mier's grandson, Marin, in a personal interview with him by the author, April 1996.
79. Minge, 9.
80. Josiah Gregg, *Commerce of the Prairies* (Max L. Moorhead, ed.) (Norman: University of Oklahoma Press, 1954), 134.
81. Dorothy Boyd Bowen, "A Brief History of Spanish Textile Production in the Southwest" in Fisher, ed., *Rio Grande Textiles,* 3.
82. Joe Ben Wheat, "Saltillo Serapes of Mexico," in Fisher, ed., *Rio Grande Textiles,* 60.
83. Ibid.
84. Ibid.
85. Minge, 18.
86. Ibid., 20.
87. Ibid., 19.
88. Ibid., 18–19.
89. Trish Spillman, "Jerga," in Fisher, ed., *Rio Grande Textiles,* 114.
90. Ibid.
91. Ibid., 115.
92. Ibid., 117.
93. Ibid., 114–118.
94. Bowen, 41.
95. Ibid., 41–42.
96. Ibid., 41.
97. Ibid.
98. Ibid., 41.
99. Spillman, 43.
100. Ibid., 45.
101. Ibid., 45.
102. Ibid., 48.
103. Wheat, 60.
104. Ibid.
105. Ibid.
106. Ibid., 58.
107. Ibid., 58–60.
108. Also see Wheat's discussion in Fisher, ed., *Rio Grande Textiles,* 62.
109. Baizerman, 44. Also see Wheat's "Saltillo Serapes of Mexico" in Fisher, ed., *Rio Grande Textiles,* 60–63.
110. Baizerman, 51.
111. Ibid., 52.
112. Nora Fisher more thoroughly discusses these blankets in her essay "Vallero Blankets" in *Rio Grande Textiles,* 97–103.
113. Baizerman, 75.
114. Ibid., 76.
115. Anonymous, *American Museum of Natural History Journal* (Washington, DC: Smithsonian Institution Press, 1912), 33.
116. Baizerman, 78.
117. Ibid., 180.
118. Ibid., 180.
119. Ibid.
120. Ibid., 181–182.
121. Ibid., 183.
122. Ibid., 1.

GLOSSARY

aniline dyes The original chemical dyes, synthesized from coal tar. Although there are now a number of chemical dye systems in place, the term aniline is sometimes used to mean "chemical" or "synthetic."

bayeta A lighter weight wool yardage cloth, woven then fulled.

bayetón A heavyweight wool yardage cloth, woven then fulled. This would be more like a modern commercial wool blanket.

beater A loom part that holds the reed and beats the weft in place.

Chimayó Rio Grande weaving style using two Rio Grande stripes and one central design derived from Saltillo elements. Many Southwest design influences are incorporated into Chimayó weavings.

churro The "peasant" breed of sheep in Spain, exported to Spanish settlements in the New World, including New Mexico.

crimp Natural curl in wool fibers.

despacio A "slow" tapestry design advances over one warp thread per round of weaving.

dovetail Makes a vertical line by having the two bordering tapestry yarn colors turning around the same warp thread.

end Warp thread.

ends per inch (epi) The number of warp threads per inch.

frazada Blanket.

fulling A process of washing and felting fabric to make it softer.

harness A frame holding the heddles, the harness is lifted and lowered by use of the pedals of the loom.

heddle A metal, wire, or string device installed in a harness through which a warp thread is passed.

ikat A resist-dye technique where yarn is tightly bound to stop penetration of the dye in predetermined places to create a pattern when that yarn is woven.

jaspes Inlaid single rounds creating a small line woven between shuttle-woven rounds, commonly found in larger Chimayó weavings.

jerga A coarse, twill-woven utilitarian cloth.

loom A frame that holds the warp threads in proper order and tension for weaving.

merino The "royal" breed of sheep, protected for many years by the Spanish Crown. It produces especially fine wool.

Moki As a variation of the Rio Grande blanket, the Moki is dominated by a rhythmic pattern of natural black and indigo stripes, with narrow bands of natural white wool. It can have tapestry designs as well. It is very similar to Pueblo and Navajo Moki styles.

mordant The material chemically bonding the dye to the wool, setting the color.

natural dyes Dyes extracted from plant, animal, or mineral sources.

paladar In English this would be known as "pick and pick." A common element in Rio Grande and Chimayó stripes.

pedals On a Rio Grande loom a weaver stands on the pedals (treadles) to lift and lower the harnesses to create the opening to pass the weft through.

pick and pick One shuttle lays down a "pick" of one color followed by another shuttle laying down a "pick" of the other color, that is, alternating picks. It creates a comblike look.

piquiete A very small diamond-shaped design element, essentially an inlaid tapestry-woven triangle, usually inserted between shuttle-woven rounds.

plain weave The simplest weave structure, a plain weave has weft yarns passing over one warp thread then under one warp thread.

plying Twisting two or more strands together.

Rambouillet The French variation on the merino breed of sheep.

recio A "fast" tapestry design advancing over two warp threads per round.

reed A comblike device, set into the beater on the loom, keeping warp threads properly spaced in the woven fabric.

Rio Grande A term for the Hispanic weaving tradition of New Mexico and Colorado. Also used to describe the striped blankets woven within that tradition.

Rio Grande Saltillo Woven within the Rio Grande tradition, these retain many elements and sometimes the overall design pattern of their more finely woven Mexican counterparts.

round After the shuttle has laid down one line of thread (pick) in each direction a round has been woven.

sabanilla A fine, plain-woven, wool yardage cloth used for bedding and colcha embroidery.

Saltillo sarape Said to be from Saltillo, Mexico, these were extremely fine and detailed tapestries consisting of a usually serrate diamond-shaped center design with a vertically structured background design and an intricately worked border.

sarape A wearing blanket, usually with a slit for the head.

sayal A coarse, plain-woven utilitarian yardage cloth.

shuttle A tool for carrying the weft thread across the warp.

tapestry Using a "discontinuous weft," that is, the weft yarn does not pass from one woven edge to the other.

Trampas-Vallero This version of the Vallero has four stars placed in the corners and one central star.

twill weave A weave construction in which wefts pass over two or more warps, creating floats that are usually aligned diagonally.

Vallero Design style identified by use of an eight-pointed star, the Vallero has much in common with the formal design of the Rio Grande Saltillo.

warp The threads running lengthwise on the loom. In Rio Grande blankets the warp is very much the underlying structure.

weft Threads crossing the warp to form a fabric.

weft-faced Only the weft is visible in the finished fabric. In Rio Grande blankets the warp is visible in the fringes only.

BIBLIOGRAPHY

Anonymous. *American Museum of Natural History Journal.* Washington, DC: Smithsonian Institution Press, 1912.

Baizerman, Suzanne. "Textiles, Traditions and Tourist Art: Hispanic Weaving in Northern New Mexico." Unpublished Ph.D. dissertation, Department of Anthropology, University of Minnesota, 1987.

Baxter, John O. *Las Carneradas: Sheep Trade in New Mexico, 1700–1860.* Albuquerque: Historical Society of New Mexico Publications Series, 1987.

Boyd, E. *Popular Arts of Spanish New Mexico.* Santa Fe: Museum of New Mexico Press, 1974.

Chavez, Fray Angelico. *Origins of New Mexico Families: A Geneology of the Spanish Colonial Period.* Santa Fe: Museum of New Mexico Press, 1975.

Connor, Seymour V., and Jimmy M. Skaggs. *Broadcloth and Britches: The Santa Fe Trade.* College Station and London: Texas A&M University Press, 1977.

Doyle, Gene. "Candelario's Fabulous Curios." *The Denver Posse Westerners Monthly Roundup* 24:9 (1968): 9.

Fisher, Nora, ed. *Rio Grande Textiles: A New Edition of Spanish Textile Traditions of New Mexico and Colorado.* Santa Fe: Museum of New Mexico Press, 1994.

Fisher, Phyllis K. *Los Alamos Experience.* Tokyo and New York: Japan Publications, 1985.

Forrest, Suzanne. *The Preservation of the Village: New Mexico's Hispanics and the New Deal.* Albuquerque: University of New Mexico, New Mexico Land Grant Series, 1989.

Gregg, Josiah. *Commerce of the Prairies.* Max L. Moorhead, ed. Norman: University of Oklahoma Press, 1954.

Lucero, Helen R. "Hispanic Weavers of North Central New Mexico: Social/Historical and Educational Dimensions of a Continuing Artistic Tradition." Unpublished Ph.D. dissertation, Department of Education, University of New Mexico, 1986.

Lyon, Fern, and Jacob Evans. *Los Alamos, the First Forty Years.* Los Alamos, NM: Los Alamos Historical Society, 1984.

Nestor, Sarah. *The Native Market of the Spanish New Mexican Craftsmen: Santa Fe, 1933–1940.* Santa Fe: Colonial New Mexico Historical Foundation, 1978.

Rochlin, Harriet, and Fred Rochlin. *Pioneer Jews: A New Life in the Far West.* Los Angeles: Rosebud Books, 1984.

Twitchell, Ralph Emerson. *Old Santa Fe: The Story of New Mexico's Ancient Capital.* Santa Fe: New Mexico Publishing, 1925.

Usner, Don. *Sabino's Map.* Santa Fe: Museum of New Mexico Press, 1995.

Weigle, Marta, ed. *Hispanic Villages of New Mexico.* Santa Fe: Lightning Tree Press, 1974.

Weigle, Marta, ed., with Claudia and Samuel Larcombe. *Hispanic Arts and Ethnohistory in the Southwest.* Santa Fe: Ancient City Press, 1983.

Wroth, William, ed. *Hispanic Crafts of the Southwest.* Colorado Springs: Taylor Museum of the Colorado Springs Fine Arts Center, 1977.

The Trujillo family (Lisa, Emily, Adam and Irvin), 1998.